STANDING ON THE SHOULDERS OF ONLINE GIANTS

7 WAYS TO USE BIG ONLINE BRANDS TO POSITION YOUR BUSINESS FOR GROWTH AND PROFITS.

FABIO MASTROCOLA

Copyright © 2014.

Register To Get Your FREE Webinar and Bonuses.

To get updates to this book and access to your FREE Webinar and Bonuses that will show you how to position and grow your business with the strategies in this book visit: **www.onlinegiantsbook.com**

Disclaimer:

The purpose of this book is to educate. This information is provided and sold with the knowledge that the publisher and author do not offer any legal, accounting or other professional advice. In the case of a need for any such expertise consult with the appropriate professional.

This book does not contain all information available on the subject. This book has not been created to be specific to any individual's or organizations' situation or needs.

Every effort has been made to make this book as accurate as possible. However, there may be typographical and or content errors. Therefore, this book should serve only as a general guide and not as the ultimate source of subject information.

This book contains information that might be dated and is intended only to educate and entertain. The author and publisher shall have no liability or responsibility to any person or entity regarding any loss or damage incurred, or alleged to have incurred, directly or indirectly, by the information contained in this book. You hereby agree to be bound by this disclaimer or you may return this book within the guarantee time period for a full refund.

About This Book

Let me start off by saying Thank You for getting a copy of my book. I wrote this book for you, the small to medium business owner, Professional, Coach, Artist, Consultant, Author, Speaker, Home Based Business Owner and Multi Level Marketers out there working day to day making a living and a difference by providing products and services as a solution to solve their community and customers problems.

In have always been of the opinion that small to medium enterprises are the lifeblood of the economies and countries worldwide and my hope is that by reading this book you will benefit by becoming more educated and aware in what is available in the ever evolving world of the digital marketing landscape. You will learn how to harness the power of digital multicast marketing and how you too can leverage (in most cases at no cost) the big brands of the internet like Google, YouTube, Apple and Amazon to name a few. You will learn the opportunity that awaits you by standing on the shoulders of these online giants and how you too can prosper.

This book represents my journey in learning how to market, learning how to promote businesses, including my own and also the businesses that I've consulted with. It represents a period of my life of over 14 years of where I've helped my own business and also clients in their businesses to really promote their business, their brand to their ideal audience and to make them attractive and trustworthy for their clients and prospective clients to engage with them and do business with them.

My Inspiration to Write This Book

My inspiration for writing this book really came from a story that I heard quite a few years ago when I first started to learn about marketing. This story actually stayed with me and it's only years later now that I get to write about it. The story I'm referring to is the story of the George Foreman Grill. This story is amazing. There are a few lessons that you can get out of this story. The George Forman Grill which has sold over 100 million grills. This story highlights the power of the celebrity, the power of having a platform (a following), and the power of endorsement.

What really fascinated me and wanted to share with you is; how you can actually stand on the shoulders of these online giants. I am going to be sharing with you how can tap into their platforms and their followers and use it to your advantage to position you and your business as the expert in your chosen market or field.

Let me share with you the story of the George Foreman Grill as I know it and how George Foreman came about to endorse this product. The concept of the grill was actually created by a gentleman by the name of Michael Boehm as a result of creating a follow up product to supersede his sandwich maker. This grill was designed to drain away fat from the food. From what I'm lead to believe the concept never really took off so it was finely pitched to a few companies with George Foreman as the proposed celebrity to endorse the product because of these three things.

One, George had recently regained his heavyweight world boxing championship, and the second thing was he was known for eating two hamburgers before every fight, and these hamburgers were fat reduced. So these two things combined with the third element, being his passion and his enthusiasm for the product made it an ideal fit. They renamed the grill the Lean Mean Fat Reducing Grilling Machine. More commonly known as the George Foreman Grill.

The grill was promoted through late night infomercials that you may have seen. It really proved to be a hit, linking George Foreman and the grill together. It really got me thinking about the power of having a platform because directly or indirectly they were tapping into those who were a fan or admired George Foreman to sell the grill.

I thought about it a little more and then I suppose I had a light bulb moment. In today's digital economy we have a lot of platforms like Apple, Facebook, Pinterest, Google, YouTube, Amazon, LinkedIn, Twitter etcetera that have made it accessible to reach the people that are on these networks. If you think that Facebook has over 1.3 billion users, you've got YouTube that has over 1 billion users, LinkedIn with over 300 million active users, Instagram with 200 million users, it really got me thinking about how no matter what business you are in, you could use these platforms to reach out, connect, engage, and build the know, like and trust factor with the audiences that are on these platforms and more importantly the audiences that are aligned to the product or service you sell or provide.

Positioning You, Your Brand And Your Business For Success

The marketing tactics I am going to share with you are powerful, straight forward to implement *(they will take some effort on your part)* and will help you position you and your business as the go to expert in your market or niche. I will show you throughout this book how to set yourself apart from your competitors, make a positive impact and possibly dominate your market. There is not one business that I know of that these strategies won't work for.

This book is going to be to the point, no fluff. It's not going to be a long novel. I will give you examples and I will write as clear as I can to help you understand the techniques and opportunities each tactic or strategy presents for your business. I hope you are OK with this?

I am also assuming that as a business owner you are honest, ethical and that the quality and the service that you provide is of a very high standard because the strategies that I am going to be teaching you will need you to have these attributes.

Why? Simply because as much as this can help you position yourself as the expert in your market or niche, if you don't provide a good quality service and product and don't put an effort in trying to satisfy your customers, this could also have a negative effect on your business. - That's my **WARNING** to you!

You will also see that I use the words like, your market, niche, target market, field, industry or audience. These terms are used to describe a sector of people you liaise with, help, sell to, educate and inform. You will see me use these terms often throughout this book.

You may see some typo's in this book. I am going to ask you not focus on my errors but on the message and the content. I am the son of two Italian immigrants and I started life as English being my second language! That's right "I speak good England!"... ha-ha.

Should you find any errors please let me know by emailing me at onlinegiantsbook@gmail.com

I will also mention the word digital marketing a few times. What exactly is digital marketing? - Here is my definition:

Digital marketing is marketing that reaches your ideal audience with your message on platforms that they are connected to and engage with devices like PCs, smart phones, mobile phones/cell phones, tablets gaming consoles and smart web enabled TV's.

These devices are used to engage and serve your audience and if you don't have presence online other than a website or a facebook page you will be left behind.

Many organizations these days use a combination of both traditional and digital marketing channels which brings me to the point that, even though we are just talking about the digital marketing in this book, it's also very important not to forget your offline marketing like direct mail marketing, business cards, flyers, telemarketing and other offline marketing strategies you may use.

Today there is an opportunity for you the business owner, coach, author, speaker, artist, consultant, professional, multilevel marketer and home based business owner to leverage the big brands and distribute your message on multiple platforms of these online giants .

Companies like Apple, Facebook, Amazon, Google and YouTube to name a few. These giant brands of the internet will give you the opportunity to use their platforms to reach their customers, providing that you provide great quality content.

Podcasting for example, it's very easy to start your own podcast you will have the opportunity to reach over 1 Billion subscribers, that's right I said billion with a "B". YouTube *(More than 1billion unique users visit YouTube each month.)* also give you the opportunity to distribute your message and reach your ideal clients and customers via your own videos. Both of these platforms have a lot of people there that are waiting to hear, watch and read your message and content, giving you the opportunity to drive them back to your business or website.

But my business is different...

I just to also dispel the, "*Well, my business is different"* excuse. I personally don't believe this to be the case and I can prove this to you. All you need to do is go into a platform like iTunes and type in your area of expertise and more than likely there is a podcast on the topic or there is a book on Amazon about what you do or a related industry. So really give it some thought. It does provide you with a great opportunity to really make yourself stand out from your competitors and throughout this book I'm going to be showing you how.

Your Opportunity

Digital marketing presents to you a wonderful opportunity to really make a positive impact in your market or niche by promoting your message, your business and / or your brand at a time when most of the world's population is connected to a mobile device of some sort. You literally have an opening to connect with your audience and literally be carried around everywhere they go in their pockets (via their smart phones) and in their homes through PC's, Laptops, Tablets and Smart TV's.

I hope you enjoy reading this book as much as I have enjoyed putting it together for you!

Warm Regards,

Fabio Mastrocola

TABLE OF CONTENTS

Register To Get Your FREE Webinar and Bonuses.	*2*
About This Book	*5*
Endorsements:	*15*
Special Thanks To	*17*
Chapter 1 Understanding Your Market	*19*
Chapter 2: Verbal Positioning	*30*
Chapter 3: Strategy # 1 - Publish A Book For Instant Credibility	*35*
Chapter 4: Strategy # 2 - Use The Power Of Video	*44*
Chapter 5: Strategy # 3 - Use The Power Of Webinars	*59*
Chapter 6: Strategy # 4 - Start Your Own Web TV Show	*67*
Chapter 7 : Strategy # 5 - Podcasting For Business	*71*
Chapter 8: Strategy # 6 - Blogging Magic	*79*
Chapter 9 : Strategy # 7 - Publish Your Own Online Digital Magazine	*86*
Chapter 10 - Create Exquisite High Quality Content	*90*
4 Bonus Chapters	*100*
Bonus Chapter 1 - Speak Out !	*101*
Bonus Chapter 2 - Media Exposure With Press Releases	*109*
Bonus Chapter 3 - Go To The People And Their Power	*118*
Bonus Chapter 4 - What's Your Service Like?	*122*
Moving Forward	*133*
About The Author:	*136*

Endorsements:

Fabio has helped my real estate business to establish strategies, systems and more importantly teach our team how to target the markets we are wanting to do business with. His easy going approach, understanding of online marketing and his ability to simplify the complex has been really valuable. He quickly understood our needs and worked alongside us to implement the strategies. I highly recommend Fabio to work with businesses that want to adapt online marketing strategies into their business.

Torrin Minutillo, Director, Diamond Realty Pty Ltd.

We engaged the services of Fabio Mastrocola for professional advice on start up business marketing strategies. His professional approach and enthusiastic personality enabled for a clear and concise communication . Fabio has a comprehensive understanding of marketing in a wide range of specialised industries. Fabio gave me excellent advice on developing strategies to analyse customer demographics and behaviours. Not only did Fabio discuss short term marketing strategies, but he produced mid and long term sales tactics in which to continually address the needs of my business and those of my clients. I have been able to employ the plans recommended by Fabio to develop my current and future client bank. Fabio's expansive marketing knowledge and his ability to communicate unambiguous business strategies makes him an invaluable asset to any business. Without doubt, Fabio's skills and knowledge has injected a positive impact into my business.

Andy Symons, Director, Pulse Medical Emergency Training Pty Ltd.

Fabio has helped our business move ahead in a forever changing market. He has fantastic knowledge of digital marketing and with that has created an online presence for our company. He is very approachable and has unbelievable ideas. Fabio has been able to provide invaluable advice to obtaining the most positive outcome for a growing business going forward.

Dino Donatelli, Director Gropak Aust Pty Ltd.

Special Thanks To:

In my life I have been blessed to have wonderful people around me. A special Thank You to my wife Rita for your support, love, your kindness and encouragement. Mamma Rosaria my awesome mum who has been a great support, you are just wonderful. My Father Italo, RIP. There is not a day that goes by that I don't think of you. I miss you, your humour and you just being around. Daniela and Roberto my younger siblings thank you for being there. I love you all so much. My extended family, all my aunts, uncles, cousins, in laws and friends you are all awesome.

I want to mention the incredible teachers and mentors that have made an impact on my business life. A special shout out goes out to Lui Donatelli, Mal Emery, Steven Essa, Mike Koenigs and Ed Rush - **Thank you!**

Chapter 1: Understanding Your Market

In this chapter we're going to talk about the most critical thing you must do which is identifying and understanding your market and your customer / client profiles. You may have heard this also called as identifying your clients' avatar. In addition to your clients profile it is also very important you also know your competitors well.

Why is this so important? Simply, because once you get into the minds of what your customers want, what their fears, frustrations and challenges are and understanding how your competitors are advertising and delivering their products or service you will be able to effectively communicate with your audience on the online platforms they frequent. You will be able to speak directly to them, show them that you understand what is needed to assist with their needs because you have taken the time to do the research. It will also give you an insight to what products or services they require and then be able to use the coming strategies to position you, your business and products and services in front of them.

Before we find out who our ideal clients are and who our competitors are in our markets or niche, I just want to talk to you about positioning. Positioning is a concept in marketing which I personally came across in late 1999 by reading Jack Trout and Al Ries book titled: Positioning - The Battle for Your Mind. Whilst I may have forgotten most of what they both taught in their book *(Time to re visit the book I think.)* I have always remembered the title of the book, especially the part - The Battle For The Mind and today with so much noise out in market places it certainly is a battle of capturing your customers minds!

It's said that positioning happens in the minds of your target market, your audience and how accurately you can describe your target market and how well you know your client profile?

Being able to define and have clarity around your target market is the first thing you need to do before you put your marketing strategy together and also very important in positioning yourself as the expert in your area of expertise.

How To Research Your Client Profile

We are now going to focus our attention on the process of really uncovering our client profile.

We are going to use demographics, geography and psychographics to really get to know our client profile. First a quick explanation of each:

Demographics: When you're talking about the demographics of people, you are looking at data such as their gender, age, marital status, their income, their occupation, the education levels, employment status, household sizes and what stage in their life they are at? *(Maybe they are retirees or maybe they are just entering the workforce.)*

Psychographics: Is concerned with your clients attitudes, values and lifestyles, how they behave and what are their situations. Like what influences their buying decisions, What are their motivations, What activities do they take part in and What are their interests. And lastly you have:

Geography: which is quite self-explanatory, where exactly are they located? Are they local, national or internationally based. Do they gather on online forums or social media platforms. If so which ones?

A Quick Story of Janet From The Local Cafe

Recently my wife and I noticed on an afternoon walk that a new cafe had opened at the end of our street. We decided to go in and try their coffee *(I love my coffee and I am known as a bit of coffee snob to my friends, family and peers.)* While we were waiting for our order we chatted to the owner, a delightful lady by the name of Janet. In our conversation I asked her why she chose to open a cafe in this location? Her response surprised me because she had done her homework, something that in my experience not many small business owners do properly or at all. She told that her and her husband researched the area and found out that the residents in the area were well established. The area was close to schools two primary schools and one high school *(there is a school next to her cafe)* and she was able to tell me that most of the population of the area were aged 35 years plus, most of the residents owned their own homes and have two income sources. Janet also studied the behaviour of the mothers of the school children and noticed that a good few of them would arrive up to 30 minutes before the kids finished school and would congregate around the school gates chatting. She noticed this happening over about a week or so and approached them, giving them a flyer advertising a coffee and cake special. Where do you think they go now 30 minutes before school finishes to have a chat? That's how important it is to know your audience and their behaviours.

OK moving on, here are list of client profiling questions:

What are their core concerns and problems? *(What is your target market's core problems?)*

What are the solutions?

What are their top 5 goals?

What keeps them awake at night?

What are their top three daily frustrations?

If you were to get into their minds and their hearts, what is it that they secretly and truly want? *(If you can work that out, you've got the key.)*

What age are they?

What gender are they? Are they mostly male or female or both?

What's their occupation?

What are their family details? Are they married? Divorced? Single? Have kids?

What are their interests?

Where are they located?

Who influences them? Are they influenced by their peers *(Do they keep up with the Jones's)*, Rock Stars, Celebrities, Religion, Politics?

Where do they go to search for information? Online, offline or both?

Do they read magazines or other publications like trade or industry journals? If so which ones?

These are just some of the profiling questions that will help you to identify and create your client profile. If you are wanting to position yourself well in your market it's important to take the time to do this research.

Here is my client profile as a result of answering these questions and using a survey:

Male aged between 40 - 55 who owns and runs a small to medium business that sells high ticket products and services. He wants a successful business and understands the value of having an online presence of more than just a website for attracting leads, more sales, profits and repeat business. He is married with at least two children, owns his own home and lives in a major city. He likes to spend available work time networking with like minded colleagues either at conferences and or seminars related to his industry. He spends his recreational time with his wife and kids doing family activities e.g.- Family holidays, as well as pursuing his hobbies typically in the water sports, boating, golf, playing tennis and travel both for business and pleasure.

He would like to take his business to the next level. The challenges he faces in his business are hiring and managing staff, cash flow, getting more clients and he is frustrated with the competition in his market .

He also struggles with time, as he wears too many hats at work dealing with the day to day running of his business that he doesn't have the time to market his business and product or services effectively. His goals are to build more cash flow, free up his time so that he can spend more time with his family and participating in his hobbies.

Ideally he wants a business that runs efficiently and in profit without him being there because he has good reliable staff and as result increased business and market share in his market or niche.

He is also into DIY, likes to purchase items online. He likes to use his computer and understands that it's a tool that can generate more business by communicating with his target audience.

He reads publications both online and offline that are both free or he subscribes to in his industry sector and watches and reads the news, and news on finance, shares and the property market. He wants to live a more affluent life for himself and family.

Pretty detailed? Can you picture what he looks like?

Here are few other tips to help you with understanding your market and identifying your client profile.

Use surveys to find out more about your customers. This can work whether you already have a data base or not. You can use a service like SurveyMonkey.com to build a questionnaire and send it to your clients via email. At the time of writing this book Survey Monkey do have a basic free option that allows you to ask 10 questions per survey and receive up to 100 responses at no charge.

Another option which is free is to create your own survey in Google Docs via your Google Drive account all you need is to register a Gmail account with Google and then send it out to your list and post on your social media platforms. Post the survey on your Facebook page or profile and other social media platforms like LinkedIn, Google Plus, Pinterest *(only post on the sites that are relevant to your target market)* and ask your friends and fans to share the post.

You can also, if you have an allocated budget advertise your survey on Facebook. Facebook is a good option because you can drill down and target your ads to your audience. Run the survey ad campaign for 3 to 5 days. Be sure to set a daily spend amount so you don't overspend on your allocated budget.

Generally speaking there's not many people I know that love doing long surveys so if you can limit your questions to 5 or 10 maximum might be an idea. Use a combination of multiple choice and text answers. Also offer them a chance to win a prize or some sort of ethical bribe to complete your survey.

You can use a "one question survey". For example:

What is the biggest challenge you are having with (insert challenge)? or What is your number one challenge you are having with (insert challenge)?

E.g. *What is the number one challenge that is stopping you from having a profitable business?*

Search sites like: Quora.com, Yahoo Answers and Askville.com on questions that are posed by clients in your market.

Search online ecommerce sites like Ebay.com and Amazon.com best sellers to see what is selling and in what category. It's also important to read the reviews on your competitors products, find out what is good about their product and what wasn't liked about the product by your target market.

Search and engage in forums and blogs in your market .See what your audience is talking about. You can find these by simply typing in your niche keyword and the term blogs or forums in Google.com.

Look at social media. For example search Facebook fan pages and groups on your topic of expertise and see what your audience is talking about. You can do this on Twitter, Google + and LinkedIn as well.

Ask your clients face to face or over the phone, connect and engage with them in conversation to find out more about them, their goals, desires, fears and frustrations.

Look at review sites like Yelp.com, Amazon reviews *(where products are concerned)* and Google reviews for customer experiences.

How Well Do You Know Your Competitors?

Let me ask you do you know who your competitors are? What are strengths and what are their weaknesses? Are there any gaps you can fill or do better with?

Make a list of the top 5 to 10 competitors in your market or niche and do an analysis on them. Find out some back ground information on them. Here are a few questions to help you know more about your competitors:

Where are their offices located? Are they local *(They may possibly have more than one site)*, national or international?

What products or services are they selling?

How do you compare on product, service, price, terms, features and benefits?

Look at your competitors Social Media, What are they talking about, promoting? etc.

Visit their place of business if possible.

What competitive advantage do they have over your business?

What can you do better than your competitors?

What do you need to do better to compete with your competitors?

Do they have an online presence? And if so, how do they market online?

Do they market offline and how and where?

What products or services are they selling?

How good is the customer service?

Do they offer a guarantee ? If so, what is it and how does it compare to your guarantee?

Shop them, what I mean is buy and use their products or services. Here you will get to experience their customer service, how they market, their selling process and how good their product or service is. Then look at how your product or service and service delivery compares and make the necessary adjustments if you need to improve as a result of your research and experience.

This is all information that you can use to your advantage. Knowing the answer to these questions will give you more clarity on how to market yourself and how to differentiate your business from your competitors. It will also give you an idea on a marketing budget for your business. Be sure to take the time to complete this exercise, it will pay off big time!

> Register To get updates to this book and access to your **FREE Webinar and Bonuses Visit**:
> www.onlinegiantsbook.com

Use Google To Keep You Updated On Your Competition

One way to keep an eye on your competition just so you know what's going on is simply to create a Google alert via Google. Just go search "Google alert" in the search engines and you will find instructions on how to set it up. It's a simple process to set up. Just enter competitor/s name in and anytime your competitor/s is mentioned on the web you will be notified about what they're doing. Google Alerts are also a great way to keep you informed on your industry and also if your name or business has been mentioned on the web.

On a final note be sure to take the time to complete this research because in the next chapter and the ones following it; I am going to reveal to you your first tool to position yourself as the expert in market or niche and you are going to need the answers to the client and competitive profiling questions. See you in chapter two.

Chapter 2: Verbal Positioning

Now that you have your customer profile bedded down from the time and effort you put in the last chapter, it's time to move to crafting a sales message that is congruent to your market.

I am going to take you through the process in this chapter and I am going to show you how straight forward it is to *"Verbally Position"* yourself as the expert. This tactic will set you apart from your competitors because I am 99% sure that they are not doing this.

Once you bed down this next method you can use it in all of your marketing including social media profiles, business cards, direct mail, your website, letter heads just to name a few places.

Ok are you ready ?

The powerful VERBAL POSITIONING method I am talking about is called your "Elevator Pitch" or "Elevator Speech" which is a short few sentences used to promptly inform a person of your profession, product, service and /or organization and its value offerings.

Elevator pitches are known to be short *(known as an elevator pitch as your statement should be delivered in the time your are in the elevator with a person approx 30 seconds to about 1minute 30 seconds)*, sharp and to the point with the goal of getting a curious reaction from the prospect that the message is being delivered to.

Think back to when you have been in a social situation like a party or at a barbeque and you meet someone new for the first time. It's always guaranteed that they will ask you or you ask them - "What do you do for a living?

The typical response will be I'm a Business Owner or I'm a Lawyer, Beautician, Journalist, etc... Can you relate? Everyone answers by saying "I'm a stating their occupation. Very ho - hum and pretty standard way of communicating what you do. It doesn't really capture the attention of the person, engage them or raise their curiosity for them to want to know more!

A Simple Formula To Verbally Position Yourself And Make People Remember You!

The simple formula for developing your elevator speech I am going to share with you now will really make a big difference when engaging with your prospect. It will build curiosity and they will remember and refer you.

Here is the formula:

You know how.......... + Well what I do is............

Let me give you an example:

Here is mine - Instead of saying I'm a Digital Marketing Coach I use:

"You know how most small to medium enterprise owners struggle growing their businesses in today's digital age. Well what I do is teach and train small to medium enterprise owners how to position themselves as the expert in their field to get more customers and create more cash flow in their business by using the power of Digital Multicast Marketing".

I then say "Would you like to know more?" If they say yes it shows they are interested. This work really well at networking events, meet ups, conferences, seminars and workshops.

Most times I get this response "How do you do that?" *(It builds curiosity).*

Let me explain the formula in more detail for you so that you can get started writing and using your own.

Let's start with the first part of the formula:

You know how - here you want to write what your clients pain points / frustrations/ dilemma's are; in my case after doing the research we conducted in chapter one relating to identifying and understanding your client profile, it was clear that my target market of small to medium enterprise owners had challenges with business growth, customer conversion, cash flow, competition and a lack of presence online *(Positioning).*

"You know how most small to medium enterprise owners struggle growing their businesses in today's digital age.

The next part of the formula:

Well what I do is - this is where you provide your solution (Teach and Train SME's) on how to use Digital Multicast Marketing and the benefits of your solution *(Position their business for more customers and increased cash flow).*

"Well what I do is teach and train small to medium enterprise owners how to position themselves as the expert in their field, to get more customers and create more cash flow in their business by using the power of Digital Multicast Marketing".

You can also use the I help/provide formula which is a little shorter but still effective. Using my example above :

"I help small to medium enterprise owners that are struggling to grow their businesses online in today's digital age by showing them how to position their business to get more customers and create more cash flow in their business by using the power of Digital Multicast Marketing".

Here are a few other examples to help you along:

Tax Accountant

"I help businesses set up compliant accounting structures that maximize their tax advantages so that they can increase their income and grow and develop a cost efficient and profitable business."

Makeup Artist:

"You know how a women's skin changes with age and it seems to take a lot time and effort to achieve that glow you once had. Well what I do is teach mature makeup workshops to show how ladies can get a more youthful and vibrant look. Would you like to know more?"

Chiropractor

"I help people suffering from chronic and debilitating migraines find complete relief using their body's natural healing powers so that they can get back to doing the activities they love."

Here is a tip: Add your elevator pitch on your social media profiles (Google +, LinkedIn, etc.). This will do wonders to make you stand out from your competitors and create intrigue with your audience. Then you can make it even more powerful by adding a call to action (CTA) to engage your prospective clients.

For example:

"I help small to medium enterprise owners that are struggling to grow their businesses online in today's digital age by showing them how to position their business to convert more customers, create more cash flow in their business by using the power of Digital Multicast Marketing".

"Call me now on (insert contact number) to discover how I can help you with the positioning your business for more customers and create more cash flow using Digital Multi Cast Marketing."

You could also ask them to connect with you via your social network or ask them to visit your site.

I hope you enjoyed that tip. Let's move on to the next chapter.

Chapter 3: Strategy # 1 - Publish A Book For Instant Credibility

The first way you can use the big online giants is to write a book and publish the book on Amazon.com. There are other platforms you can this on as well but we are going to focus on using Amazon. You have probably read the title of this Chapter and said Whaaaatt!! Write a book! Are you crazy - I can't do that! I haven't written since I left College or University!

Please stay with me. I want you to take a deep breath, listen and suspend your disbelief for a minute or two because I am going to share with you an awesomely powerful and straight forward way of writing a book in and how you can get it done in less than 60 days.

I will also let you know of a fantastic resource that will show you strategies on how to position yourself as the expert in your field and profit even before your book is published.

To start with, I want to touch on how simple it is today to establish yourself as an author and position yourself as an expert in your field by writing a book. With platforms like Amazon's Create Space and Kindle Direct Publishing platforms, gone are the days where you have to wait two years or so to become a published author. The old way of publishing your book took a long time and was quite involved. You had to write your book, send your book to publishers with a proposal, or have an agent act on your behalf of which I am told that to engage an agent you would already had to have written a successful book *(Lets' be honest If you are like me then, I had no hope of that happening!)*. Then you wait to hear from the publishing house or your agent to see if your book has been accepted to be published.

As I have mentioned thanks to Amazon it's not like this today. Amazon's platforms provide you with a great opportunity to pen your book. I have heard it said that everyone has a book in them and I totally agree. Why? Simply because we all have different experiences in life, expert knowledge and a message to share . Just think of the happy, sad, funny or inspirational stories you share with your friends, family, customers, colleagues and people you meet in your life.

In this chapter I am not going to show you how to write a fictional romance novel or a Stephen King contemporary horror book because for one I am not that creative and two I have never written these types of book before.

I have though; written this book on the knowledge I have on digital multi cast marketing by helping small to medium business owners market their business online. I am going to show you how to do the same in your area of expertise by outlining the steps .

12 Reasons Why Writing Your Book Will Benefit You and Your Business

Position yourself as the authority and expert in your field, niche or market.

You and your business will stand out and set yourself apart from your competitors and others in your market or industry.

You will get instant credibility.

It will put you and your business in pole position to attract new clients and income.

A book is a business card on steroids. Imagine meeting a prospective client at a networking event and they ask you for your business card but instead you hand them a copy of your book. Don't you think they will be impressed by that? Do you think they will bin your book as most people do with business cards? It will only demonstrate to them that you are an expert in your field and the value you have given to them in the time you've had contact.

The opportunity to become an Amazon best seller in your niche or market may sound like a long shot and probably hard to fathom but it's very possible.

A powerful lead generating tool - Your book will open doors to more opportunities and customers /clients.

Your book will create more exposure to reach a larger audience because you are more visible on a platform like Amazon which is available worldwide. This is especially great for Educators, Coaches, Business Owners, Entrepreneurs, Artists, Professionals, Authors and Speakers. It may lead to opportunities to help customers from all over the globe over the world wide web.

"I think that is so cool!"

A book can get you publicity. You will have the opportunity to get exposure on radio, TV, all online and offline media and be interviewed or just have your business mentioned or featured.

Get you speaking engagements; another way to demonstrate your expertise and authority in your market.

Create other streams of Income - Speakers, Authors, Coaches, Consultants and Educators can turn their book into training courses, webinars, paid seminars, workshops, membership sites and coaching programs.

Leave a legacy for you, your family or your business.

Inspire others to do the same.

The length of your book doesn't have to be a long 300 to 400 hundred page novel. It can be shorter, I have seen Kindle eBooks that are 50 pages or less.

I think what's most important is that you write clearly to communicate your message and also provide quality content people will enjoy, can use and also consider to hire you for your services or visit your business (online or offline) to buy your products.

Let's Get Started Creating Your Book

You have two options to creating and publishing your book and they are that you write it yourself or you outsource the writing of the book. I am going to take you through the process on how I wrote and published this book. It's by no means the ultimate way to do it but it's a simple and a relatively quick process to publishing your book. I am all about simplicity and getting things completed.

If you want to look into having the book researched and written for you, you can check these sites out:

iwriter.com (writing, and formatted for Kindle)

Fiverr.com (editing and cover design)

odesk.com (writer, editing and cover design, formatting)

guru.com (writer, editing and cover design, formatting)

Prices will vary and it's important before you hire a writer, editor, cover designer etc.. that you check out their ratings and look at the work history, feedback, reviews and that they are in your price range.

A Simple formula you can use to come up with content for your book is the 10 x 10 formula. I learnt this from Mike Koenigs, whom I consider to be marketing and automation genius. Simply think of the 10 most frequently asked questions (FAQ's) you get asked by your customers and write them down. Then go through them and answer them. The next step is write down 10 questions that your customers should ask (SAQ's) and answer them also. You can record this process and have it transcribed. This process is great way to get content for your book.

OK, let me walk you through the process I used to write and publish my book. Most of the tools I used to create my book are free. The first thing I did was to open a word document on my PC. If you don't have Microsoft word that's no problem as you can use Google drive (formerly known as Google docs), all you need is a Gmail account to get access. If you are a Mac user the program is called Pages. Alternatively you can use a free program called

Open Office and use the word processor called writer.

I then downloaded a program called Audacity, which is a free audio editor and recording software available for both PC and Mac and available at:

http://audacity.sourceforge.net/.

The next step was to create an outline which included:

My purpose and objective of writing my book. Next I wrote a table of contents and under each heading or chapter name I typed in point form the content I was going to cover in each chapter.

I also included A "moving forward" Chapter which summarises the content in your book and included a call to action for you to visit my site and subscribe, connect with me on social media or get them to call your business for more information.

I then plugged in my microphone *(I use an Audio Technica ATR 2500 USB microphone).* A simple headset with a microphone is fine. I then fired up the Audacity software, clicked on record and starting talking freely on the points I had in front of me in my outline. I recorded one chapter at a time and then downloaded and exported the recording in mp3 format from audacity and saved it on my computer in a file titled book. *("I know how innovative of me!")*

Tip: It's important you set a plan and the time aside to record your content every day. Don't try to do it all one sitting you will get tired and possibly become a little frazzled.

Do it when you are fresh.

Once you have completed recording all of your content have it transcribed. I used two sites Fiverr.com and Rev.com to get this task done.

I then created the title and subtitle of my book and designed my cover on a piece of paper so that I could send it to a designer on Fiverr.com to complete and make it look great. You can use any of the other services mentioned above to complete this task.

Once I received my transcription back I proof read it and added more content and wrote a special thanks section, about the author, disclaimer, about this book, and rephrased the content where it needed improvement. I then sent my draft to be formatted correctly for Amazon on fiverr.com. After the necessary changes were made I uploaded it to Amazon Kindle Direct Publishing following their guided process and bingo I was a published author.

If you want your book available for sale as a paperback you will need to format the book so it's compatible for publishing through Amazon's Createspace. The formatting for Kindle and Createspace is different. You will also need to invest in having a front cover, back cover and spine created for your book. You can go to the outsourcing sites to get this done. Amazon's Createspace also offer this service.

You can then order copies of your own book for just a few dollars each and have them shipped to you by Amazon. You now have a business card on steroids you can use to open doors for new business and as a lead generating tool.

> **Register To Get Your Free Resource Guide** that lists all the tools and programs to help you with getting your book published. Visit: **www.OnlineGiantsBook.com**

8 Simple Suggestions For Promoting Your Book

Claim your Amazon authors page and fill in your Bio *(include your website address and include your photo)*. It also gives you an option to upload a video. You can add a video of yourself telling the reader what your book is about or create and upload a mini commercial, known as a book trailer. You can use a simple software like Animoto to do this or simply out source it. You can also link your blog and twitter account to your author page.

Use the 0.99c pricing strategy *(For Your downloadable Kindle Book)* and promote your book on your social media and to clients via email, customers, family and friends and ask them to buy your book and review it online. You want to aim to get four or five star reviews.

Write and submit a press release about your book on its launch date. (Be sure to read my chapter on getting media exposure using press releases.)

Email your data base letting them know of your book.

Create a book trailer as mentioned above and publish it on video platforms like YouTube, Vimeo and Daily Motion with a link in the description area pointing back to your Amazon listing or the book's own website.

If you like, you can create a webpage or website dedicated to your book.

Write a blog post about your book so that your clients and those who visit your site are aware of your book.

Amazon owns a company called Audible.com which sells audio books online. Here is an opportunity to have your written word spoken and recorded and turned into an audio book. Again you can record and read it yourself and upload your book to audible.com or simply outsource the process to the sites I have already recommended.

Start promoting your book before it's even published. As I promised in the beginning of this chapter I promised a fantastic resource that will give your great tips and pointers on how to promote your book and attract business before it's even finished. The resource I am talking about is available at MissionPublishing.com. This is John Eggen's site, a master at book publishing and has done it for many years. Sign up for his complimentary mini course he has some great strategies on how to promote, get exposure and attract clients before your book is even published. It's absolute gold.

I also recommend my teacher Mike Keonigs and his book Publish and Profit available at PublishAndProfit.com for great content and excellent value.

Final Thoughts

Today you have been given an opportunity to write a book and use it to position yourself as an expert in your market by standing on the shoulders the DIGITAL GIANT known as Amazon. Take the time to do it. Set yourself a goal to be a published author in 30, 60, 90 days or less. Take action. Don't over agonise over it just get it done. You will be glad you did!

Chapter 4: Strategy # 2 - Use The Power Of Video

In this chapter we are going to cover how video can be used in your business to increase your exposure to your market, help you communicate your message to your audience and help with establishing you as the authority in your chosen market or niche.

Video is a great way to give you a competitive advantage and in this chapter I am going to show you the various ways to use video in your business.

We will be discussing and touching on areas like online video and different formats you can use, offline video, video production *(and No you don't need to be a Steven Spielberg to do this.)* I will point you in the right direction and give some simple ideas that are easy to implement.

So Why video ?

Well to start off with we have all been conditioned to watch TV whether it was the news, MTV, your favourite soaps, sports or late night movies. We have also seen the transition from free to air television to cable TV and now on demand and instantly downloadable shows of all genres all accessible via the net and on portable devices like laptops, smart phones and tablets. *People love video!*

So why use video for your business? Here are 5 very powerful reasons :

Firstly, video is an excellent media for building rapport with your audience. Video is engaging, it's visual, it has audio and you can use it to demonstrate and connect with your customers.

Secondly, using video to promote you, your business or your brand sets you apart from your competition. It's a powerful differentiator.

Thirdly, video helps you build your credibility in your market and it gives you a wonderful opportunity to have people get to know, like and trust you.

The fourth reason it increases the exposure of your business or brand and works 24/7 for you.

And finally, video ranks well in major search engines like, Google.com, Youtube.com, Bing.com and Yahoo.com to give your business more exposure and drive visitors back to your website and place of business.

Here are some very inspiring facts about why you should use online video marketing :

FACT ONE : 96% of consumers find videos helpful when making purchase decisions online.

Nearly three quarters are more likely to purchase a product or service if they can watch a video explaining it beforehand.

FACT TWO: 73% of all US adults are more likely to purchase after watching an online video that explains a product or service, making it the next big sales tool for small businesses.

FACT THREE: Most shared video content was humorous content at 94%, heart warming at 91% and then educational at 89%

FACT FOUR: Globally, IP video will represent 79 percent of all traffic by 2018, up from 66 percent in 2013.

(Source: Cisco.com -Visual Network Index, www.animoto.com/blog/business/small-business-video-infographic/ - 03/13/14)

17 Ways To Use Video For You, Your Business And Your Brand

Let's look at some powerful ways you can use video to market your business. You can use it to:

Educate your audience on what you do and how you can help them.

Provide quality content about what's happening in your industry, sector, market or niche. Don't be scared to give away your best content as it will only strengthen your bond and engagement with your customers and prospective customers.

Create a sales video on your product or service offerings. (Remember to add a call to action i.e. Act Now by calling us on.... to place your order, visit our online store or enter your details in the form provided below to have one of our friendly staff members help you with x..)

Here's an example that you are more than welcome to use to model your message on:

Hi my name is John Smith from the Plumbers Gallery located in Malaga, Perth ,WA. We have been providing our *plumbing service for both domestic and commercial customers since 1972. No job is too big or small for the Plumbers Gallery, whether it be a blocked drains, water hammering problems, hot water system break down and repair or gas leaks we've got you covered. Our experienced team are on hand to deliver an expert and a responsive service to deal with any plumbing issues you may have. Our qualified plumbers will treat you with courtesy and leave no mess behind. Call to speak to one of our friendly staff now on 555 555 555 or visit our site at www.plumbinggallery.org and request your free no obligation plumbing evaluation valued at $150.00.The number again is 555 555 555. We look forward to hearing from you. Bye for now.*

You can use video to answer frequently asked questions (FAQ"S) - Remember the 10x10 formula we discussed in Chapter 3 - 10 FAQ's and 10 SAQ's (Should Ask Questions).

You can use videos to create a knowledge base for staff training.

Demonstrate your product or service. Shoot a video showing how your product, service works. You can use screen capture software like Jing, Snag it or Camtasia if you need to record your computer screen- this is great if you are demonstrating software.

Client testimonials and case studies. Having your clients go on record giving you a video testimonial is great social proof. Interview your clients for case studies. You can do this using your smart phone, camcorder or Google Hangouts On Air using your webcam.

Content creation: interview other experts in your market online using Google Hangouts to create more content for your audience. This works well for video podcasts.

Use video to do sales presentations live, interview people for jobs using video and webinar platforms like Google Hangouts, YouTube Live, or Go to meeting.

In your email marketing and messages to increase open rates. I remember a former boss using this tactic in sending us his season's greetings for Christmas one year. He had in the subject title: *A Video Message For Fabio.* This got my attention as I saw my name mentioned in the email subject line. Then in the body of the email he had embedded a picture that said click here. When you clicked on the picture it went to a video with his message. Pretty Powerful and I guarantee that few of your competitors are doing anything like this.

Burn your video sales message or sales presentation on DVD, Blue Ray Disc or USB (Branded with your company's details if possible). Use it to market your services when people ask to send out information. In our last federal election one of the candidates, Clive Palmer used DVD's to market his political message by mailing a DVD to households in all the capital cities and regional centres here in Australia. He is a prominent business figure (a Mining Magnate) in Australia and if I recall correctly he started his own independent political party and entered the campaign race late. This marketing strategy helped him win a seat in our parliament. He was able to get into the homes of Australians via his DVD and deliver his message.

Use it on your social media platforms and ask your connections to share your video posts. Who knows a person of influence may connect with you, or maybe it will get shared around so much that it will go viral.

Use video on your landing pages and websites to engage visitors by welcoming them to your site and encouraging them to subscribe, listen to your sales message or other quality content and practical tips you have to share on your site.

Create an infomercial for your business, like you see on late at night TV.

You can use video when launching new product or service.

Start your own web TV show. This works well if you are a Artist, Coach, Consultant, Speaker or Author. You can use services like livestream.com, usstream.com, YouTube Live or Google Hangouts *(I cover this in another chapter.)*

Repurpose your content and convert any blog post, article you have written or audio podcast into video.

There you go, just a few ideas you have available to you on how to use video to promote you and your brand.

Distributing Your Message On Popular Video Sharing Platforms.

There are many online video sharing platforms on the web and you can easily search for them by doing a search on Google. I am going to reveal to 3 sites that I use to upload my videos to. They are YouTube, Daily motion and Vimeo. The reason I like these sites is that they seem to be liked by the search engines and rank well with some basic video seo *(Search Engine Optimisation)*.

Here is a quick overview of these three platforms:

YouTube has over 1 Billion active users each month. It has over 100 hours of video uploaded every minute. Millions of people subscribe to YouTube channels each day and the number is set increase four times over the next year. YouTube is available in 61 Countries and across 61 languages.

Vimeo on the other hand is not as popular as YouTube but is growing. It has 100 Million users and 170,000,000 unique viewers worldwide and there were 4.9 Billion videos streamed in 2013.

Then we have Daily motion The 32nd most visited website worldwide as of 2012. It has 2.2 Billion video views per month and 116 Million unique visitors per month. Even though it's French company, 85% of our audience is outside of France.

(Source: https://www.youtube.com/yt/press/statistics.html, https://vimeo.com/about/advertisers & wikipedia.org)

Recording & Producing Your Video - Your Options

Now that we have gone through why and how you should use video in your business and the three video sharing platforms I recommend you get started on. It's time to produce a video. I am going to give you some solutions on how to do this and keep to my promise of showing you that you don't have to be Steven Spielberg to do this.

Preparation is the key. Take the time to think about what your goal of the video is. For instance are you going to script a video to sell your product or service or educate your audience?

The next step is to think about how you are going to communicate your message:

Remembering your client profile we identified in Chapter 1. You will have to envision you are communicating to them as if they are there sitting in front of you and then write a script and learn it in preparation for the recording of your video.

Here are your options when it comes to creating and recording your video:

Firstly, outsource it and hire the talent to record your video if you don't want to do it or

Secondly, do it yourself.

Outsourcing it will depend on your budget and how far you want to take the video production process. Here are some suggestions:

You can engage a local video production company to do it for you.

You can also go to your local college or universities that run courses on Film, Television and Screen Arts and hire a student to help you *(this can be very cost effective)*. Also if you are not keen on being in front of a video camera you could hire a drama or journalism student to do your talking head video.

Search outsourcing sites like fiverr, odesk and guru.com for talent that can help you with your video production.

Should you decide to do it yourself you can produce your video three main ways. They are:

You in front of the camera, also known as a talking head video, similar to a news anchor or reporter who is on location reporting today's news.

Screen Capture where you can present your information by recording a power point or keynote presentation on your computer screen using a software tool like camtasia, snagit, Jing or Screenr. This process can also be used to demonstrate how to use a software online or to build up a knowledge base of staff training videos for a business.

Slide Show Video - Here you can upload images to a slide show video software like Animoto to produce a slide show video that is synced to music *(make sure it's royalty free music)* .

What you could also do is hire a voice over talent on fiverr to record your script in mp3 audio format and then upload it and let Animoto produce your video.

For your talking head video you can simply use your smart phone to record your videos. The quality on these phones are of a very high grade. I have seen people record videos using camcorders, tapeless camcorders like the Flip or Kodak Zi8 and Webcams that all record in HD quality.

Here is a tip for you, If you are having trouble remembering your script you can upload the script to what's known as an online teleprompter via your tablet, position your tablet behind the camera and you can then read straight off the screen of your laptop or tablet. Here are some free online teleprompters you can check out:

cueprompter.com

easyprompter.com

freeteleprompter.org

Remember to speak clearly, confidently and with intention.

Now you have recorded your video download it (mp4 format works best for the web). If your video needs further editing and you have never edited before, I recommend you have the editing done by an outsourcer this will save you a lot of frustration. But if you have edited video before knock your socks off and do it yourself.

Video SEO - Making Your Video Findable On The Web

I mentioned at the beginning of this chapter that search engines love to display videos in the search engine results pages (SERPS). Google loves to display YouTube Videos on the first page on the web results as well as under the videos tab. I am going to show you some basic video seo - (search engine optimization) to give your video the best chance rank on page 1 of Google *(This will depend on how competitive the Keyword your trying to rank for is).*

Here is the process I use and I have included a **Bonus Free Guide** that goes into more detail and you can access by registering at: www.OnlineGiantsBook.com

Step 1: Optimize Your Video File Name

Optimize your video file name to the keyword you are trying to rank for . For example I ranked a video for a high end luxury home builder in my home town of Perth, Western Australia. In my keyword research I found the term Perth Luxury Home Builder was being searched. I named the video file Perth- Luxury- Home- Builder.mp4. You can also use an underscore_ in place of the dashes.

I did this by simply right clicking on the video file and renaming the file to Perth-Luxury-Home-Builder.mp4

Step 2: Upload Your Video To YouTube - You will need to set up a you tube account to upload your videos to. Over the past year, YouTube have encouraged you to connect your YouTube channel with a Google+ profile or page to access it's new feature offerings. *(Make Sure That before you upload the video it is set on public setting, this will allow anyone to see your video.)*

Step 3: Include Your Keyword In Your Title **(Very Important)**

In my example it was simply: Perth Luxury Home Builder

Step 4 : Write A "Descriptive" Description

Start the description with your keyword at the beginning and then add your website address in this format http://www.yoursite.com (The "http://" makes the link clickable and will direct your viewer to your website or landing page). The next step is to write a good description including your keywords and related keywords. *(A word of warning don't over use your keywords in your description you don't want to be seen as keyword stuffing.)* Write about 500 words and include links to your social media platforms and include call to actions like asking them to visit your site or subscribe for updates. Also at the end if you are a business write your:

Company's Name

Address

Contact Number

in this order.

Step 5: Add Your Keywords In Your Tags .

Add your primary keyword first and then other related relevant ones.

Step 6: Fill in The Advanced Settings Area:

Simple and straight forward to do. Be sure to include your location and date of recording. Also remember to select the right category you want your video to feature in, i.e. Education, How To and Style etc.

Step 7: After you have uploaded and published the video:

Copy the video url from YouTube it will look something like this www.youtube.com/watch?v=Ch52Tv145QE and paste it at the bottom of your description area.

Use the same video url to let the search engines know that the video exists by going to a service like pingler.com. Here you put your keyword in the title area, paste in your YouTube video url, select the relevant categories and hit ping. This process will have your video indexed by the search engines.

Share your YouTube video on your relevant social media Pages, Facebook, Twitter, Google+, Linkedin, Pinterest etc.

Post your video to your blog or website and ping the blog post url using pingler.com.

Social Bookmarking. I use social monkee to bookmark my videos. You can outsource this process on fiverr.com. Just make sure that they book mark your video over a period of 10 days like they do at socialmonkee.com.

Step 8 : Submit Your Video To Other Video Sharing Sites.

Here you repeat the process and upload and optimize your video on Vimeo and Daily motion sites. At the end of the video description remember to include the YouTube url. This will link back to your YouTube video and help you achieve a better video ranking in the search engines for your YouTube videos.

This process will take a bit of time to do if haven't done it before. Once you have done it once or twice you will get better at it and hence take less time to complete this task.

Mike Koenigs has a very powerful tool that will automate this process and more. It's called Traffic Geyser 2.0. I strongly advise you check it out.

Optimize Your YouTube Channel

It's important to optimize your YouTube channel as well. (This applies to your Vimeo and Daily Motion Channels.) Here are few tips to help you along.

Channel name

There are two schools of thought when it comes to picking a channel name for your YouTube. The first is to use your business name or secondly what your business does, for example, Perth Luxury Home Builder. In my experience what I have seen rank is naming your channel your primary keyword if it's available. This makes sense to me because if

I was searching for a luxury home builder to construct my home in my city of Perth I would input that search term into Google.

Channel description

Your channel description should accurately describe what your channel is about. Use your main and relevant Keywords in your description. Make it interesting and engaging so that those reading want to know more about your channel. Ask them to subscribe to your channel or connect with you on one of your social media platforms. Complete the *About Section* by adding all your links to your websites and social media accounts. Engage in the discussions and comments on your channel as well - This shows activity and engagement which is what YouTube loves.

Channel Art

It' important to catch the eye and create engagement of visitors to your channel with great visually appealing channel banners. Have one designed for you by a graphic artist.

Create Playlists - this is a great opportunity to keep the visitor on your channel longer. Playlists will be a great way to display your 10 x 10 FAQ' and SAQ's as discussed earlier. Also playlists are very effective when you share them on Facebook.

I know we have covered a lot in this chapter and I don't want you to feel overwhelmed. I want you to take the time to re read this chapter or comeback to it. Take some time to consider how you are going to implement video for you, your business or your brand.

I want to finish this chapter with a story:

Back in 2002 my wife Rita and I started a dance school in my home town of Perth called Salsa Down Under. As the name suggests we taught salsa dance classes. It was fun and I met a lot great people with whom I am still friends with today. My wife Rita (a wonderful dancer) and I decided to record a learn to salsa DVD and we ended up with an interactive DVD called "*Learn To Dance Salsa In Your Living Room*". We sold it to students and online and it did reasonably well. Today it's still available but I have put the lessons online into a membership site. You can check it out at letsdancesalsa.com. I had a lady come to my class one evening to join our dance classes. She was pleasant and very friendly. I was taking down her details and chatting to her like I did with everyone. After a few minutes of chatting she turned around and said" *Fabio - I feel like I have known you for ages*" to which I replied, "*Really, why is that ?*" She said, "You have been in my lounge room for months." She had been given a copy of our DVD as a present and was practicing her steps at home before she built enough courage to take a salsa dance class. She then said that she chose our dance school because of the way we instructed on the DVD which ended up her entrusting us to take her through her salsa dancing journey. I shared this story to illustrate to you how powerful video is to help you create that know, like and trust factor.

See You In The Next Chapter

Chapter 5: Strategy # 3 - Use The Power Of Webinars

In this chapter you are going to discover how to leverage the trust and reach of the online giants, Google, YouTube and other platforms like Go to webinar to help build instant credibility, authority and create exposure in your market by doing webinars. The technology these brands offer you has made it easy and cost effective to start your own online broad cast whether it be a webinar, Google hangout, web TV show or live streaming event.

Breaking Through The Clutter

I heard recently that the average person is exposed to over 8000 marketing messages a day through all the different types of media radio, TV, bill boards, infomercials, bus stop advertising, online advertising, direct mail advertising, newspaper advertising and the list goes on and on. We are bombarded by all these marketing messages. Can I ask you though, how many of these marketing messages do you remember? Not many, right? Using webinars and having your own web TV show *(covered in the next chapter)* will give you more exposure and set you apart from your competitors in a massive way. Why? Simply because these forms of communication use video to create engagement and done correctly will enhance, for the better your know, like and trust factors.

Webinars

What are webinars? Put simply webinars are interactive seminars delivered online from anywhere where there is an internet connection. Whether you are looking to educate and grow your business; I have experienced webinars work for all types of businesses; large corporations, small to medium enterprises, professionals, speakers, coaches, authors, in multi level marketing, government and one person home based businesses. They are fantastic way to deliver your message and connect with your market.

Platforms Used To Deliver Your Webinars and Live Casts.

Webinars and live casts are delivered on platforms such as gotomeeting.com *(paid service)* and you can do similar on Google Hangouts an instant messaging and video chat platform developed by Google and is free to use. Go to meeting has been around since 2004 and it is very trusted brand for delivering online events like webinars. There are many options for every budget, all you need to do is search.

Why use webinars ?

Adding webinars to your marketing mix is something I suggest you do. They are straight forward and easy to run. The other reason is that they work and webinars done correctly will actually expand your business.

Here's a list of the benefits for using webinars in your business (*In no particular order*):

They build trust and rapport with your audience, they engage people *(webinar attendees)* to get to know you.

Webinars are a great way to demonstrate and talk about your product and /or service.

They can be used as a lead generation tool to bring people into your funnel and build your customer data base.

Webinars are a great way of helping you set yourself apart and help you dominate your market or niche *(Positioning)*.

Great way to test if there is market for your product or service before creating a product and service.

Save You Time, Save You Money and Make You Money.

Increase conversions. Most websites will convert 1-2% of the traffic that visits your website. Webinars that are delivered correctly will convert at 10% plus.

Repurpose content. You can leverage the content you present in a webinar and turn it into information products, articles, podcasts, blog posts, books and training modules.

Webinars allow you to present to one person or a group of people. Webinars are an excellent selling platform and gives you the opportunity to sell to one or many people who attend your presentation.

Leverage; you can present to others peoples list, gaining more exposure, building your database and sell to another persons or company's database.

You can record your live presentations and automate them having your webinars available for replays using software like The Webinator found at www.webinator.biz or a Wordpress plug-in by the name WP Webinar www.wpwebinar.com. This is fantastic leverage for you as you get the opportunity to run your webinars you have already presented 24/7 and if you have more than one webinar presentation it's even more powerful because it's like having a sales force bring you in leads and sales on autopilot.

Great for creating a knowledge base for training purposes.

How To Use Webinars In Your Business

Here is a quick snap shot on how you can use webinars in your business. You can use it as communication tool for running meetings with staff, customers and clients locally, nationally and internationally. Webinars are an effective selling platform as well as using them for interviews if you are hiring staff or interviewing an expert on a subject. Webinars can be recorded and stored which makes them an excellent way to develop training content, create answers to frequently asked questions that can be uploaded on your website to assist your visitors and save you time in customer support.

Webinars, as I have already mentioned are a wonderful positioning tool where you can share your knowledge and expertise to your audience. They are a great way to educate and place you in the minds of your audience.

How To Monetize Your Webinars

"A lot of people are doing webinars... only a few know how to monetise them effectively."

Steven Essa x10effect.com

I wanted to share with this quote by Steven Essa who is a leading expert on how to use webinars effectively in your business and someone who has been an influence and teacher of mine over the last 5 years. Steven's quote reigns true in that not many people know how to maximize and monetize their webinars. I am going to share with you some models on how you can make money for your business using webinars:

The Demo Model - Present, demonstrate and sell your product or service on a live webinar.

Info Product Model - Create and sell information products like a paid training series, information delivered in a membership site where you can earn recurring monthly income.

List Builder/ Lead Generator Model - Giveaway a valuable webinar you have put together yourself or one where you have interviewed a known expert in your market in exchange for some ones name and email address.

Coaching Model - Use your webinars to teach your students in your market delivering quality content, question and answer sessions to help them learn, achieve and grow. This can be in the form of a high end coaching package which can be delivered through a membership site. I have seen this work in countless industries from business coaching to forex trading and everything in between.

Do It For Others Model: There are a lot of people, businesses, speakers, authors that one; don't know how to use webinars and two; are so busy working in their business that they don't have the time. You can offer them a service where you organise, create, promote and even deliver the webinar for a fee or percentage of sales.

Joint Venture Model - Here you can find and contact people with databases in your industry and ask them if they want have a joint venture arrangement where you can present your product or service to them and their database and agree to split the profits with them. It's win win. They get extra revenue and you get to leverage their list and also profit. *(This strategy works really well if you have a great product and no list or a small list.)*

6 Steps For Doing Your Webinar / Live Cast

Step 1: Schedule A Date And Time For Your Webinar / Live Cast using Google Hangouts or webinar platform like Gotomeeting.com. Decide how long your webinar is going to be 60 or 90 minutes?

Step 2: Attract and Promote Your Webinar / Live cast . Here are some suggestions on how:

Email your list.

Announce and share your webinar on your social media account and ask your, fans, followers and friends to share the registration link to your webinar.

Create an event in Facebook and invite your friends and fans to attend your event.

Create a YouTube video, a mini commercial with the link to your webinar. *(Also upload the video on other video sharing platforms like Vimeo and Daily motion.)*

Announce the webinar on your blog/ website.

Write and send out a press release about your webinar.

Paid Traffic - Use Facebook Ads, Bing Ads and YouTube Ads (Upload a short video that asks them to register for webinar).

Leverage the person your interviewing to promote to his or her list and social media followers.

Create a power point slide (embed a clickable link to register for the webinar) with a catchy title (include Keyword) promoting the webinar and upload your slides to SlideShare.net.

Promote it on classified ad sites like Craigslist, Back Page and Gumtree.

Create Your Presentation Slides - Using Power Point, Keynote, Google Docs etc.

Step 3: Deliver Your Presentation

Deliver great content. In your introduction include a stick strategy, which gives the attendee a reason or an incentive to stay till the end of the webinar. For example if you are running a webinar on *"7 WAYS TO USE BIG ONLINE BRANDS TO POSITION YOUR BUSINESS FOR GROWTH AND PROFITS.* You could say that later on in the webinar you will give them or show them how to access a free video or guide on 4 powerful bonus strategies that compliment the 7 strategies I am already teaching on the webinar.

Step 4: Make An Offer / Have A Call To Action - If you are selling your product or service, make your attendees an offer. If you aren't selling anything on your webinar think of call to actions to build on the relationship you have made with your webinar attendees. Ask them to subscribe to your website for more updates and trainings or simply connect with you on social media.

Step 5: Follow up - Send out an email with the replay details to your database that registered and didn't attend. For those that did attend keep communicating with them via email, especially if you have made an offer with an expiration date. Let them know there is only 24 hours to go until the special offer expires.

Step 6: Automate - Use a replay software like the webinator or wpwebinar to make your recorded webinar or live cast available and keep promoting it to prospective customers via the tactics explained in *Attract and Promote Your Webinar / Live Cast* section above.

Webinars are a fantastic way to sell, get your message out there, set yourself apart from your competition and automate your business. Get on board using the power of webinars to launch, promote and position your business for success.

Chapter 6: Strategy # 4 - Start Your Own Web TV Show

Starting your own web TV show is a great way to own your position in your market or niche. It's never been easier to start your own show and you can do it in a very cost effective manner.

All you need to do is deliver great content that educates and entertains your audience. Web TV shows work across many industries and markets. I have seen web TV shows on topics from real estate, health, small business marketing, photo shop tips and tricks, MLM, computer programming, and gardening to name a few.

So Why Start Your Own Web TV Show? The Benefits And Opportunity.

There has never been a better time to start your own online TV Show. Some of the benefits you can expect with having your own Web TV Show are exposure worldwide and data base development and at the moment it's untapped and little competition. Having an online TV Show will help you define your position as the go to expert in your market. You can launch your web TV show on Google, using Google Hang Outs On Air *(which is free to use)* and your webcam making it very cost effective to start.

I hear you saying, *"I can't do this".* I am going to ask; What is stopping you? Are you scared? Don't know what you are going to talk about?, You think it's too expensive to start?

Let me help you get some clarity around your objections. I have just mentioned that you can get started using Google hang outs and your webcam so cost shouldn't really be a factor. As long as you connect with your market or niche and deliver great content you can build on your show as time goes on and you have more resources available.

Gary Vaynerchuk made 1000 episodes and developed a global following on his Web Show called Wine Library TV. You can deliver your show using this simple format. Take the time check out Gary's show .

You have your knowledge and expertise to share with your audience. There is a lot of content in your head, you just need to get it out. One way to do this is to simply write the questions and answers to commonly asked questions you have received and then write down the answers and build the content of your shows around them. Another way is to interview other experts and thought leaders in your field on your show. This will help you gain credibility and elevate your standing in your market as well as connect with brilliant people other than yourself.

11 Quick Tips To Starting Your Show

Decide on your shows format. For example how long is the showing going to be, how many segments in the show, are you going to be the sole host or are you going to have someone as co-host. Show lengths can very I have seen shows ranging from 3 minutes to 30 minutes plus.

Plan and script every show. Know what you are going to cover and how long each segment is going to run for.

Come up with a name for your show. Be sure to make the name memorable.

Buy a domain name for your show i.e. www.yourshowsname.tv or www.yourshowsnametv.com and build a website for your show. *(I recommend building it on wordpress.org.)*

Use Google Hangouts to record your show as the search engines, especially Google like them.

Be consistent and focussed to produce a show either every week, two weeks or every month.

Keep the audience engaged in your show. You can do this by running polls, surveys, competitions or simply asking them to email with their most pressing question and answer it on the show either live or include it in your next episode. This will also help in your content creation for your future shows.

Embed your web shows on to your website i.e. Use keyword rich titles for your episodes for better search engine optimisation *(visibility in the search engines)*.

Promote your show and it's episodes on social media , your database, by writing and submitting a press release online and offline, and creating video teasers on YouTube, Vimeo and Daily motion to drive more visitors to your show.

Always include a call to action in the beginning and end of your show asking them to connect with you on social media, subscribe to your show and or channel or take advantage of your offer.

Make your web TV show so good that your audience keep coming back for more.

Having your own web TV show is a great way of educating your audience and developing a strong relationship with them by providing valuable content. Your web TV show will also provide you with wonderful opportunity to reuse and repurpose your content by stripping the audio off the video and uploading to podcasting platforms like iTunes, stitcher or sound cloud etc. You can also have the audio or video transcribed into text and use it for articles on your blog, on article sites like ezine articles or article base or content for your next book. This is leverage, it will save you time and distribute your content on other popular sites on the web and in turn driving more visitors to your show, remembering web TV shows are global and who knows where your best clients will be located. Now that's exciting! As your show grows and you build a base of targeted viewers you can then attract advertisers and sponsors for your show.

So hop to it... Start your own Web TV show. I look forward to watching it.

Chapter 7: Strategy # 5 - Podcasting For Business

What is podcasting? Podcasting is the distribution of multimedia files (such as audio, videos and PDF's) over the internet for playback on mobile devices, personal computer, laptops, or internet enabled TV's.

Podcasting is increasing in popularity and an excellent way to quickly create content to get free traffic, leads and sales by partnering with online giant Apple to start your own online radio or television show that can be listened to or viewed by thousands on their mobile phones, tablets, desktop or laptop computer or Internet enabled TV's .

Tap Into Over One Billion Podcast Subscribers

Apple's iTunes platform will put your podcast in front of 1 Billion podcast subscribers. The beauty is, Apple gives you this opportunity at a no charge. Why? Simply because, Apple, like the other online giants understand that keeping their customers engaged on their site or platforms will allow them to engage more with their own brand and the longer viewers and listeners stay on their site the more chances they will have to purchase music, TV shows, books, subscribe to news stand magazines and more. This is win, win, win; that is a win for Apple as it keeps its customers happy with purchased or free content, entertained and updated, a win for you and your podcast show as it allows you to engage with an audience even if you don't have a single listener or viewer to start off with and a win for the customer as they get the content they are searching for.

Why Podcast ?

Like we have discussed In the previous chapters it is about positioning, setting yourself apart from your competitors and keep you top of your customers minds. Podcasting will do this for you, your brand and your business. It's another vehicle to help you do this and it works if you are a local, national or international Business Owner, Speaker, Coach, Author, Consultant, Artist or Professional.

Podcasting is also a very powerful medium in that it allows you to engage with your audience to a stage where you are connecting with your subscribers on a personal level yet broadcasting to a mass audience of possibly thousands of subscribers. *"Read those few lines again!"*

Podcasts are a great free source of traffic. You can use your podcast episodes to drive targeted traffic to your website by mentioning your site in your podcasts in your introduction and at the end of your podcasts of every episode - encouraging listeners to visit your website or to subscribe *(opt-in)* for updates of new shows. iTunes also give you a page to promote your podcast, including a description and a link back to your site.

Entrepreneur On Fire is a podcast show by John Lee Dumas. Each episode brings you a successful Entrepreneur who shares their journey, their failures and their successes, and much more. I saw an interview with John not too long ago. John's podcasts are responsible for driving over 2000 unique visitors to his website Entrepreneur On Fire every day, THAT'S 60,000 NEW VISITORS A MONTH. How awesome is that?

Having your own podcast show gives instant credibility by leveraging a popular and trusted brand such as Apple and it's iTunes platform. People will also be more inclined to trust your podcast show because of your connection to Apple.

Podcasting can also increase your exposure by showcasing your expertise to the worldwide media. As it stands today you will find the big media and news channels worldwide with their own podcast shows on iTunes. It is known that iTunes acts as a search engine for these media organisations to find content for their shows by searching for experts on topics their shows or news topics cover. I have seen small to medium business owners, speakers, authors, coaches, consultants and professionals be interviewed on news bulletins, business, finance and current affair shows locally, nationally, internationally on radio and TV. This happens because there is a shortage of good content out there and the media will search online for experts to interview or give their take on a related topic that is prevalent in the news at the time.

Podcasts offer flexibility and convenience. They are available on demand. They are mobile. You can access your podcast by your pc, laptop, all mobile devices and smart TV's and I believe if it hasn't happened already in cars allowing you to listen or watch podcasts when and where ever you like.

Podcasts are also a great way to make your viewers or listeners aware of your product and service offerings.

Video Podcasting Vs Audio Podcasting

A question I get asked is, "What format should I use for my podcast show, video or audio?". My answer is to this question is to find out what other shows in your niche are doing first and then decide. If you find that most of the shows are video, you can follow the trend and do the same or you can do the opposite and produce an audio podcast show. I learnt this from Ed Rush. Ed has a very successful podcast called The World's Greatest Fishing Podcast.

As the title suggests it's a show all about fishing. When Ed was deciding on which format to use he found out that there were no audio podcast shows on fishing and hence decided to deliver his show using audio. The World's Greatest Fishing Podcast and reached #25 on iTunes, got major sponsors and built a list of over 25,000 in less than two months.

You also need to ask yourself which one of the formats are you going to be more comfortable with to get started doing your podcast show. If you decide to do a video show and want to keep it simple you can use Google Hangouts On Air to record your show using just your webcam. If you decide on doing a audio show you can use a free audio editor and recording software called Audacity available for both PC and Mac to record your show. You will want to invest in a good quality microphone as it's important that the quality of your audio is of a high standard.

Tips For Starting Your Own Podcast Show

Decide on your shows format. Is it going to be audio or video? How long is the show going to be?, How many segments in the show?, Are you going to be the sole host?

Are you going to have someone as co-host your show?, Are you going to interview guests on your show? What content are you going to cover?

Show lengths can very I have seen shows ranging from as little as 7 minutes to over an hour. I would say a show in range of 15 to 25 minutes is ideal.

Plan and script every show, know what you are going to cover and how long each segment is going to run for.

Come up with a name for your show. Be sure the name of your show is memorable. *(Use keywords that describe your show in the name of your show.)* For example if you are a builder specialising in commercial property construction you might call the show "The Commercial Construction Tips Show." *(Tip: Think about what search terms, other than your business name your audience would type into Google to find your business.)* Also if you specialise in a geographical area add the city town or state in the title.

Create your show's cover art graphic. The graphic art dimensions has to be 1400 x 1400 pixels and in JPEG or PNG format. You can outsource this to a site like Fiverr.com.

Buy a domain name for your podcast show and build a website for your show to upload your episodes to. Alternatively if you have a website create another tab and name it podcasts and upload your podcast shows.

Store your episodes on Amazon's S3 hosting service it is very cost effective. It will cost you a fortune if you store your shows on your website hosting account.

Use Google Hangouts to record your video podcast show as the search engines, especially Google like them.

Be consistent and focussed to produce a show either every week, two weeks or every month.

Content is KING - Be sure to deliver excellent content that will educate your audience. Don't be afraid to give away your best content this will build trust with your audience.

Keep the audience engaged in your show. You can do this by simply asking your audience to email you with their most pressing question and answer it on the show in your next episode. This will also help in your content creation for future shows.

Promote your show and it's episodes on social media, your email list, by writing and submitting a press release online and offline, and creating video teasers on YouTube, Vimeo and Daily motion to drive visitors to your show.

Always include a call to action in the beginning and end of your show asking them to connect with you on social media, subscribe to your show, opt in to your site and or channel or take advantage of an offer.

Make your podcasts so good that your audience keep coming back for more.

Your podcast should be a content rich and a pitch free zone.

Record 5 episodes before you launch your podcast and upload all 5 as different shows. This will show that you have more than one episode and show that you are serious about podcasting on your topic.

Once you start to build your following here are 3 ways you can monetize your podcasts:

Build a list, capture their name and email by sending them to a squeeze page to build a data base. You can then market to them, promoting your own products/services or affiliate products.

Find sponsors for your show and charge them to advertise on your podcast show.

Repurpose the content of your shows and turn the content into a Kindle book, audio book you can sell or a news stand magazine that people can buy a paid subscription to.

I want to leave you with a time saving super tip. I learnt this when I made the transition of putting my learn to salsa DVD online. This is pure leverage. I call it my three in one move. Are you ready? Ok, lets' say you decide to record a live video podcast using Google Hangouts. What you can do after the your podcast episode is have the audio extracted from the video and the content of the video transcribed into text format *(this can all be done by outsourcing it to a service like fiverr or odesk)* and convert it to a PDF your listeners can download with your audio podcast. You can then upload the audio to your iTunes podcast channel and other platforms like stitcher radio and sound cloud. You will have your video podcast available on your YouTube channel and you can also embed the video podcast on your own site. Remember you can also download the video podcast from YouTube and distribute the video podcast on other video sharing platforms like Daily motion and Vimeo with a subscription link to you iTunes podcast show.

I can't stress enough how powerful podcasting as a positioning tool can be for your business, brand and the opportunities it will open up for you. This is one strategy that is really straight forward and easy to start. Get started podcasting today!

Chapter 8: Strategy # 6 - Blogging Magic

In this chapter we are going to talk about how to use your blog to brand and position you as an authoritative expert in your market or niche.

So what is a blog? The simple answer is a blog is a type of website that is used for posting entries. The word blog was coined from two words web log. A blog is used to post dialogue. Blogging is the act of posting these dialogues with your audience and it gives the opportunity to use "your voice" to connect with your audience, providing real value by keeping them informed with market updates on product and services and topics that are current in the media and relative to your audience and industry. Having your own blog gives the opportunity to respond to these topics with your perspective or opinion on them. Blogging is also a wonderful platform to build and strengthen your relationship with your customers and your audience by answering any questions they may have, showing off your expertise and also a very effective platform in that it allows you to provide advice and solutions to your audience's challenges.

How Blogging Will Help Your Business

Having a blog for your business is something today that is expected by your customers and audience and that's why this form of online media has become an important piece of your online marketing. On the other hand not having a blog may give the impression to your customers and audience that you are out of touch and unavailable to them.

Remember it's about being connected and engaged with your followers.

I remember a mentor of mine, Mal Emery, a great marketer based here in Australia asking the audience at one of his seminars if we wanted to know the secret to being a marketing expert in thirty seconds. Everyone in the room put their hands up to find out what this "BIG" secret was. We all waited in anticipation for his response. His reply was simply: "Ask them what it is that they (your audience) want!" By engaging with your audience on your blog this is exactly what your blog will allow you to do.

Your blog will provide a quick and easy way to effectively communicate with both your customers, your employees and prospective audience and as mentioned previously, used properly will help you, your company and your brand build solid relationships, trust and goodwill with your customers or clients, your audience and also as important with your employees.

I have consulted with quite a few businesses who have had a website with no blog as part of their sites menu and also with businesses that haven't got a website let alone a blog. Adding the blog component if you have a website is straight forward , just contact your web designer they will be able to assist in having a blog set up on your site. If you don't have a website I recommend you use wordpress.org (which is free) to build your blog (and website) with. If you want to do this yourself, there are plenty of tutorials online that show you how to set up a website and blog.

I personally use wordpress.org and have built sites for small business clients using this platform also. It is an excellent platform as it provides you with plugins *(little software programs that carry out different functions for your site)* you can download to make your site and site's content functional, interactive, secure and found by the search engines.

There are many blogging platforms you can use, Blogger.com being one which is owned by Google. Simply search for " blogging platforms" in your search engine of choice to find one that suits you, even though in my opinion wordpress.org is the best to use whether you are a beginner or an advanced blogger.

PLEASE NOTE: Wordpress is a publishing platform that comes in two forms: the fully hosted WordPress.com, and the self-hosted version available at WordPress.org. You will want to set up the self hosted version,WordPress.org where you will buy a domain name and hosting which is the space that you rent out to hold all your files with content and other applications online in cyberspace.

I was recently consulting with a client, who is a realtor in my home town of Perth. I was conducting a basic marketing audit on his website. I noticed that he had some great content that would be very useful and provide great value to his readers on his site. They were topics relating to residential and commercial selling, leasing and property management. The only thing was that the articles weren't delivered in the form of a blog. My client had purchased his website as an off the shelf product back six or seven years ago. The technology used to build his website was no longer supported by the company and hence couldn't add a blog to his site. What we have decided to do is to create another blog site using his company name and adding the blog at the end of it, i.e. *(yoursitenameblog.com).*

How To Drive Traffic To Your Website With Your Blog

The beauty about having a blog is that it gives the opportunity to get attention and exposure via the search engines and social media platforms to help you drive visitors to your site. In this section I am going to give some suggestions on how to achieve this.

The first thing to do is make sure your blog is optimized for the search engines. This simply means that your site is findable when someone searches for your business name or search phrases that are relevant to your businesses product or service offerings. This involves the use of keyword rich and relevant keywords in your title tags both for your site and blog posts, the header tags and good keyword and related keywords on your posts and descriptions. I know this all a bit geeky but it is important as it will make your blog and blog posts visible on the net to your prospective customers. SEO (Search Engine Optimization) expert Brian Dean has a great explanation on this topic which is easy to read and understand available on his site Backlinko.com, just search for the term "on page seo" on Brian's Site.

Write informative, engaging and high quality content blog posts. The blog should provide useful information and solutions for your audience. Don't be afraid to give away your best content for free. It will only strengthen your relationship with audience and build that know, like and trust factor.

Here Are 4 Tips On Creating And Posting Content For Your Blog:

Write the content yourself and make sure the quality of content is high, in that it will provide solutions, tips and information to your audiences problems.

Interview an expert in your niche, record the interview and then embed the video or audio into your blog site.

Outsource the writing to a service like iwriter. *(You can have good quality articles written at reasonable prices.)*

Turn old blog posts into audios and videos and vice versa.

Use multimedia in your blog posts. Don't be afraid to mix it up and use video, audio, pictures and info graphics in addition to text. These modalities increase engagement and interaction with your audience. Using multimedia increases the chances of your visitors sharing it to their connections on their social media accounts .

If you are writing a post and only using text and maybe an image write an article that is about 500 words in length using relevant and related keywords in your blog. This will help your site get listed on search engines. And remember if you are including a multimedia element like a picture, video, audio or info graphic to name them with the relevant keyword or keyword phrase you are trying to rank your post for. This is because these multimedia files can rank in the search engines on their own. Think of Google images!

Consistency will drive more traffic to your site. Decide how often you are going to post on your blog. Is it going to be once, twice or to three times per week or once a month?

Once you decide commit to writing a blog post in line with your selected posting frequency.

Here's a quick tip: You can use wordpress to create your posts and then schedule the posts to be released in the future. Pretty cool hah?

Have You Heard Of Guest Blogging?

Guest blogging is a strategy that some of the biggest brands in the world utilise often. So what exactly is guest blogging? Guest blogging is where you as writer or creator of your own blog writes a unique content rich post on another blog or site that has a similar target audience but may provide different or complimentary products and services to what you offer.

What normally happens is that the blog post will have your details i.e. your name and a link back to your site. Most sites you guest post on will also have a social sharing button which again will allow your post or article to be shared on the readers social media and possibly drive more visitors to your site .

The other benefit of guest blogging is that it will position you, your business and your brand as an authority in your market or niche. This is because the blog owner is allowing you to write a post or article on his blog and connect with his readers who will see it as an endorsement of you.

You can simply search for guest blogging opportunities via the search engines. You can simple go to your search engine of choice; Google, Bing or Yahoo and type in your keyword related to your industry and the term "guest post".

For example: Let's say you are an expert in real estate investing. You simply go to Google and type into the search bar real estate investing guest post or real estate investing guest post guidelines. Google will then return to you all the sites that have had guest posting on them. You can then check the site and the articles out.

If you find that after researching their blog and the content on their site that they are in line with a unique article that you can write then contact the blog owner see if he will let you write an article for his or her blog. Don't be offended if they say no - move on to the next.

I don't have to tell you that your article for their site has to be of excellent quality and appeal to the blog owners audience. Being mediocre won't cut it.

OK, lets' move on to the next chapter. You will like this "out of the box "idea!

Chapter 9: Strategy # 7 - Publish Your Own Online Digital Magazine

Have you ever thought of publishing your own online digital magazine? If the answer is yes then you are going to find this chapter very interesting and you will see how you can find and create content on the fly and also use content you have already produced to make your digital magazine.

Why publish a digital magazine?

Publishing a digital magazine will help enhance your own credibility and establish yourself as a leader in your field. You have the ability to get in front of your ideal customer anytime and anywhere via their mobile devices- tablets and smart phones. They will probably be carrying your content in their pockets and carry bags and listening, watching and reading your messages whilst they are commuting to and from work on public transport, at home, in the waiting rooms of Doctors surgeries and virtually anywhere, ready to digest your content.

Publishing a digital magazine also allow you to build a platform that you can use to not only reach your audience but engage with them in an interactive manner. That's right, you heard correctly" in an interactive manner!" More on this in a moment.

Platforms like Apple's newsstand, Google Play newsstand and sites like ISSUU have really levelled the playing field in being able to publish your digital magazine and connect with your audience without the exorbitant costs. Imagine having your magazine, one that you control and one you can expose to millions upon millions of eyeballs. That's exactly what these platforms will provide for your magazine. These platforms give you an opportunity to build a tribe, and a customer list.

I mentioned earlier that your digital magazine has the ability to have interactive elements within the magazine. You can embed videos, audios, pictures, polls and surveys, lead capture forms and affiliate links. Having these interactive elements at your disposal will do three things. Firstly create engagement and have your voice heard by your market. Secondly build your following and trust with your audience and thirdly give you opportunity to monetize by way of selling more of your products and services, affiliate products and services and your magazine subscriptions. I have seen people sell their magazines on monthly or yearly subscriptions by enticing people to subscribe to a free issue of their digital magazine and then up sell them with what is known as an in-app purchase to a paid subscription. Take a look at the iTunes store to see how this works. There are a variety of businesses ranging from publishing businesses, small to medium businesses, large corporations, Speakers, Authors, Coaches and MLM's using this platform across thirty six categories.

Creating Your Content

I go through the various methods of creating your content in Chapter 10.

As I mentioned in the beginning of this chapter you can get your hands on excellent content for free as long as you are willing to put the time in to search for it. You can find content on article directories sites, video and audio sharing sites like Ezine articles, YouTube and Sound Cloud for example. For those of you that are familiar with Search Engine Optimization (SEO) there is no penalty for having duplicate content in your digital magazine publications like there is on the internet.

In addition you can re-use and repurpose content you have already created in your podcasts, interviews, videos, articles and blog posts for your magazine.

You can contact the article writers and ask for their permission to publish their articles or simply publish the article and include the resource box, which credits the writer as the source of the your content.

Remember, don't let your standards drop make sure that with every issue you have great quality content that will help your readers. The length of your magazine issue is entirely up to you. At minimum I would you suggest five to six articles, add a few relevant videos and or audios to embed in your issue and of course excellent quality graphics and pictures as well. Be sure to check out other digital magazine publications in your area of expertise to see what content they include, how they display it and what their magazines cover design is like. Do they use the interactive elements we spoke about earlier?

Publishing Your Digital Magazine

Publishing your digital magazine can be outsourced. Just search some of the outsourcing sites like odesk, fiverr or guru dot com to see if there is some one that can help you publish your online magazine. Here you can get your cover created and your content put together.

When publishing your content it needs to be converted to a PDF file and then uploaded to an app publishing platform that format and publish your magazine via your developer accounts for Apple and Google Play *(You will need to register for these and pay the associated costs of $99.00, a yearly fee for Apple and $25 for Google.)* This is needed to submit your digital magazine to Apple Newsstand and Google Play Newsstand. There are a few publishing platforms out there. Here are two that I recommend you consider. Magcast.co (*For publishing on Apples Newsstand and owned by online marketing genius and nice guy Ed Dale)* and Appsmoment.com for publishing on both.

Alternatively if you'd like to learn how to publish your own digital magazine you can check out courses on Udemy.com.

Give this strategy some thought.

Chapter 10: Create Exquisite High Quality Content

In this chapter we are going to cover the second most important ingredient (after identifying your client profile) and that is creating high quality content that speaks directly to your audience. Providing high quality content will instantly set you apart from your competitors, educate and engage with your customers and standout as the authority in your market.

Creating content is also about finding your voice in your market and infusing it with your personality and demonstrating the passion you have for your market or industry. The key to producing quality content starts off with having the right mind set and wanting to provide massive value to your market by providing content of the highest standard.

In my experience those who provide consistent high quality targeted content to their market and customers are the ones that tend to prosper. Don't be afraid to give away your best content. This will only create more trust with your audience. It's about educating your customers on how you can help them. which will in turn keep you and your business in their mind as the go to person in your market or niche.

Benefits of Creating Quality Content

OK, let's look at the major benefits of creating high quality content. The first benefit is the engagement factor that high quality content has on your readers, viewers, listeners when they visit your site, YouTube video, podcast show, webinars or web TV shows, read your blog posts, info graphics, pictures and social media posts.

Engaging content will keep your audience on your web properties longer meaning that you will have more of an opportunity to connect with them to build trust and have them join your mailing list, buying your product or engaging your service offering. The other benefits of high level targeted and engaging content that solves your customers needs is that you will start to get the attention from the search engines. This is particularly powerful if you repurpose the same information in different modes, like video, audio, text, info graphics and images for example. It has the potential in going viral when shared on social media platforms, video sharing sites and audio sharing sites creating links back to your site driving more visitors and hence also improving your rank in the search engines and dramatically improving the chances of your expertise being found.

What Type Of Content Should You Create?

As mentioned in a previous paragraph your content creation efforts should be targeted to your market and speak to your client profile like you are having a conversation with them one on one. Your content should inform, educate, entertain, provide solutions to their problems and deliver massive value.

These ingredients are part of a recipe of gaining trust and building a mutually beneficial relationship with your audience. In addition it's a good idea to create evergreen content for your market or industry. Evergreen content is content that is time tested and will be still be valuable in months and years to come. Some examples of evergreen content are how to guides, resource guide for your industry, glossaries, tutorials and testimonials. For example drawing on my experience as a former salsa dance teacher I could write a "how to PDF", video or audio guide Titled: *"How To Learn Basic Salsa So that Your Are Never Stuck For Another Dance Again"* The reason I know I can do this is that salsa dancing basic steps are the foundation of dancing salsa well and they have not changed in the 15 years I have been dancing and teaching salsa.

Let's Look At Some Content Creation Strategies

There are many ways to create content that is engaging and that establishes you as an expert in your field and drives more visitors, leads, sales, referrals to your business. Here are some ways that I have found to be effective.

Interview An Expert Model

Let's start by interviewing an expert in your market. Think about a person who is an influencer or thought leader in your market and someone that lends credibility to your industry. This is a simple process to carry out. Simply contact them and ask them if you could interview them for your podcast show or web TV show to show case their expertise. You can use software like Google Hangouts, Skype, Go To Meeting or free conference call dot com to interview them and also record the call.

Taking it a few steps further let's say you interviewed your expert using Google Hangouts, you now have the interview in video format and you can extract the audio from the video and also have the video transcribed into a text document. This a great strategy to create your own information product and it's exactly how I created my learn to salsa dance course.

It also allows you to repurpose the content for your blog, publish it on video and audio sharing sites, social media, your audio podcast show, or as an interactive element for your newsstand digital magazine distributing your content all over the world wide web.

The other benefit of the interview an expert model is that the more authoritative figures you interview in your market will also elevate your status and have you seen as an expert as time goes on. Of course it's important that you are consistent and that this isn't a one shot strategy. An idea might be that you write down all the people you would like interview in your market or industry, this can also include customers and clients you have helped in the past and create a content creation calendar. Frequency combined with great content is the key!

The Get Interviewed Model

This is the reverse of the interview an expert model. Here you can put yourself forward to be interviewed. You can contact bloggers that are authorities in your market to interview you. You can contact the owners of web TV shows and podcast shows and ask if they would interview you. You can get the attention of local, national and international media through writing and sending out press releases. I used the press release strategy locally to promote my dance school and the results really gob smacked me. From a simple press release I was interviewed on local radio station and got a write up in two community newspapers and the result was 106 new customers in 24 hours. (I will cover the story on how I did it in the your bonus chapter: Media & PR).

Other sites you can check out are ExpertClick.com this is where you can register yourself as an expert in your field and will provide the opportunity to connect with the media. Expert Click is a paid service and does require reasonable investment and help a reporter (HARO) www.helpareporter.com connects experts with journalists looking for their expertise.

The 10 By 10 Formula

I learnt this strategy from Mike Koenig's who I consider to be a marketing and automation genius and person who I consider a mentor. The 10 x10 formula (actually known as 10x10x4) is a great way to create content and help you extract the knowledge and expertise you have lodged between your ears. It is a simple and straight forward process of writing down and answering the most frequently asked questions by your customers and the top 10 questions your customers should be asking about your products or your service. *(Books have been written using this model it that powerful.)*

Ideally you can record yourself on video answering your questions. If you are not comfortable with having your face on camera you can simply make some slides on power point or keynote and use a screen recording software like Jing, Camtasia or Screen flow to record your video and then convert it to audio and text (articles, reports, guides etc.) and distribute the answers to your questions to video sites, audio sites and article sites for more exposure.

Let's say you created your content *(i.e.10 FAQ's &10 SAQ's)* and decided to distribute it out to two video and two audio sharing sites you have forty videos and forty audios educating people on what it is you do and how you can help them. This is great exposure for you, your brand and your business.

The third part of Mike's formula is recording 4 videos. The first video is what's known as the get more info video and can be attached at the end of every video you have created. This is where you send them to a lead capture page, where the second video invites your visitor enter their name and email address to get all of the twenty videos you have created for them. The third video is a simple thank you for signing up and letting them know that they will receive an email with a link to all videos for them to watch. The final video will be sent via email a few days after promoting your business, your services or products. The process doesn't take as long as you think and it's worthwhile because I doubt your competition is doing this. If you really believe you don't have the time to do this you can outsource the process.

Also as a quick side note check out Mike Koenig's automation software Traffic Geyser 2.0. This software, has everything you need to have you, your business, your brand be seen, read heard and found. It's distribution power is unrivalled. It has all the tools you will ever required to market your business. I can't speak highly enough of this software tool.

Here are some other content creation ideas:

Find successful blog posts that have already been written in your market and have a track record of success and improve on them. Then promote your content where your ideal target market and community hangs out, i.e. social media networking services and forums etc. I learnt this strategy from Brain Dean at BackLinko.com check it out it's called the skyscraper method.

Use Google Keyword Search Tool, known as keyword planner. Simply type in your main keyword related to your market or industry and look at other related terms to inspire and brainstorm topics for content.

A quick content creation tip is to develop mind maps outlining the content you want cover and simply speak it into an audio recording program like audacity or simply record a Google hangout.

If you have your own Facebook group or are part of someone else's community you can get inspiration from what members are talking about and turn those ideas into content.

Set up a Google alert to keep you in touch with topics on what is happening with your market or industry. Here you will be alerted to any web content that is related to your industry. It's a great tool and free to use. You want to submit your name, business or brand so that you can be notified if you are mentioned on the web. Another service that is similar to Google Alerts is Feedly.com. Feedly is a news aggregator that stores all content that is available on the web for your market, niche or industry in one location for easy viewing.

Repurpose your content. Turn successful blog posts into videos, audios and info graphics, press releases and vice versa. Remember the web enabled mobile devices and the big online giants have the functionality today to get your messages found, heard, seen and read by many. Use it to your advantage to promote your brand and your business.

Again if you want to leverage your time you can outsource this process by hiring a Virtual Assistant or finding talent to assist you on sites like odesk and fiverr.com.

Invite guest bloggers that are aligned to your market or niche to write and post content on your blog. Your association with the guest blogger will bring more exposure to his or her followers.

How To Make Your Content Engaging

It's important to remember that you are in the promotion business, you are looking at getting your audience's attention. That is why your goal when you are creating content is to make it engaging for your audience. Remembering that you are there to educate, connect, inform and build trust with them. You can engage your audience by asking them to submit questions they may have on topics you are covering that relate to your industry and share the answers with your community. This can be done on live casts like webinars or online via your blog. One way of keeping your audience's interest is to run polls, surveys and contests. You can also share stories and case studies about the experiences you have had and or your customers or other industry leaders have had in both business and life.

We have all learnt from listening to people's experiences. It's important when you are communicating with your audience to speak to them on a personal level, with passion and as if you are talking to a member of your audience one on one. Use buzz words and jargon that is aligned to your industry. Create your content so that it's available in different modalities; video, audio, text and graphics. This increases interaction and encourage your audience to share your content as well.

How To Use Your Created Content

So finally I am going give some ideas on how to leverage and use the great content you have created. The content you have created can be formatted into a report, white paper, guide or online and offline lead generation magnet. As an example; let's say you are an Injury Lawyer who helps people with compensation claims after they have been in a motor vehicle accident and you have been interviewed on a podcast show about the ins and out of claiming compensation for a road accident a person has been impacted by, you can get the audio recording and have that interview transcribed into lead magnet report with an attention getting title like *"The 7 Things You Should Know Before Claiming Motor Vehicle Injury Compensation".* People who are searching for this information can download it directly from your website by filling in the name and email address or you could have the audio put on a CD and have the report and CD mailed out to their home. You have captured their contact details and can now start a dialogue via email or telephone with your prospective client increasing your chances of moving them along the process from the information stage to a free consultation and then hiring you as their Injury Lawyer.

You can also use your content to create an Ebook, Kindle book or paperback. Again let's use the example that you run a web TV show or podcast show interviewing the thought leaders in market or industry after a few interviews you will have ability to create a book on your topic of expertise and self publish it to platforms like Amazon or Apple's Newsstand Apps.

Your content can also be submitted to article directories, podcast directories and video sharing platforms as previously discussed and can be reused for social media posts and blog posts as well. Your content can also be turned into information products, online study courses and content for membership sites. It can be used in newsletters, you can use it in your email content and press releases.

In closing out this chapter, I think you now understand why creating excellent content is king and what it can do for you, your business and your brand. Creating quality content will open up many opportunities for you to gain more exposure in your market.

Creating content is about working smart and not hard through repurposing. The strategies we have covered in this chapter are some ideas to get you started.

Please remember you don't have to do it yourself there are talented people on outsourcing sites that can help you as well as software to save you time. I encourage you to set time apart to work on your content strategy and commit to developing your content marketing calendar.

4 Bonus Chapters

The next four chapters are other ideas I want to share with you that will compliment the strategies we have shared in the book so far. These ideas will help you in cementing you and your business as the dominant authority in your market.

Remember to sign-up for your **FREE Webinar and Bonuses!** Simply visit:

www.OnlineGiantsBook.com

Bonus Chapter 1 - Speak Out !

This chapter is the first chapter of four bonus chapters that I am going to include in this book and it has to do with public speaking and how to use speaking to grow your audience and position yourself as an expert in your market or industry.

My goal for this chapter is to give you some guidance, encouragement and tips on how to prepare, present, engage your audience and profit as a speaker. Now I understand that this maybe uncomfortable for you but it's doing the uncomfortable things that make you grow in life and business. If you are like me, you probably weren't born a speaker and probably would never of thought of using it as strategy to position you, your brand or your business as an authority in your market.

You may be surprised to learn that to become a good speaker or presenter you will need these four things; a voice, be able to speak a language; meaning a working vocabulary and grammar, something to say and willingness to express your ideas to others. The good news is that you have been using these tools for years as it's part of how we humans communicate through what's called conversation. The only difference is when you are speaking in public you are not speaking to one person but a group of people. As a quick side note when I am talking about public speaking it also includes delivering presentations via webinars, live stream, hangouts, podcasts and web TV shows.

Public speaking can open up a world of opportunities for you. It can broaden your horizons through personal development, influence, and advances in your profession and in your industry.

Understanding Your Audience

Ok lets dive into preparing your presentation. The most important element of public speaking or doing a keynote presentation is to firstly to understand who you are talking to. The more you know about your audience, the better you will be able to connect and engage with them on your presentation topic. You will also understand how to adapt your presentation and content so that you can deliver a presentation that resonates with those that attend your speaking engagement. You will be able to get information from the organisations hosting your speaking gig.

Some questions to ask the organisers are:

Who are the listeners? What is general age range? What is the gender ratio of male to female? Ask about their educational backgrounds and occupations or professions. Where are the located *(geography)*? What do they want to get from your presentation? Are they there to learn? Would they like case studies and statistics on your topic? Is it compulsory they attend? Are they there to have fun?

If you have time and the organisers of your speaking gig agree you can send out a survey asking the attendees what they would like covered in your presentation. What is the size of the audience and venue and which venue the function is being held at?

Design Your Presentation

Once you have identified your audience you are now ready to narrow your presentation based on your listener's interests and needs you have identified when doing your research you can now develop the content you are going to cover in your presentation .

When designing your presentation it is important to know what your objective of your presentation will be. Is the purpose of the presentation to inform, to educate, to entertain, or to persuade. *(You may have more than one purpose for your presentation.)*

Remember to give your best content away in your presentation to enhance the know, like and trust factors. Take in to consideration the amount of time that has been allocated for your presentation and design your presentation to fit within the limit.

Presentations that inform offer accurate data, objective information, findings, and on occasions, interpretations of these findings. Those that educate, teach the attendees on a process, procedure or strategies based on the information provided in the presentation. The presentations that entertain provide pleasure and enjoyment that make the audience laugh or identify with delightful situations. Finally, presentations that persuade and encourage the audience to take a certain action, like lead them to make a buying decision on the speakers products or service offerings by appealing first to their logic, demonstrating proof, and then to the audiences emotions.

Organising Your Presentation

A simple way to organise your presentation is to have it set out in three parts, the introduction, the content, and the conclusion.

The beginning of your presentation is essential. It gives your audience their first impression of you, your topic and your purpose. You will want to grab your audience's attention .

Here are few suggestions to do this :

Use a what's in it for me statement (benefit driven for the audience). Let's say you are a financial planner. Your opening statement could start something like this; *"I am here for one reason and one reason only and that is to show you a step by step plan for retiring wealthy - Guaranteed".* That would certainly grab my attention. A statement like that certainly packs a punch, don't you agree?

Another way would be to use a startling statement or statistic. For example, (staying with the financial planning theme) *" Soon To Retire Baby Boomers Are In The Worst Physical Shape Of Their Life - Will Their Retirement Funds Be Able To Cope With Increase In Medical Bills"*

You can also start with an interesting story whether it is emotional, humorous, enlightening, or intriguing will grab the attention of your audience. The story can be factual or made-up. It can be a personal experience, or it can be something you have read or seen on TV. For example, *"An interesting thing happened to me whilst making my way here to speak to you today."* or *"The first time I tried to ask my wife to marry me... etc."*

These examples are certainly more engaging than "Today I am going to talk about (insert your topic here.)"

The Introduction

An effective introduction has three distinct parts:

The opener, this is the first sentence. Like we have just discussed in the examples above. The opening should be short, interesting, and appropriate to the topic. Then we simply:

State the title of the speech. Say it directly as: "I have been asked to speak about (insert your topic.)" E.g. "I have been asked to speak to you about Financial Planning." The third part is briefly explaining what you will be covering in your presentation. For example :"In today's presentation I will be taking you through the 5 steps to retiring wealthy"

Organizing The Content of Your Presentation

Here is where you organise your main ideas, the content and provide visual (Power Point or Keynote slides) supports. Include good quality graphic, photos and images. It is said that 85% of all information is taken through the eyes and 80% of motivation is optically stimulated.

The body of your presentation is the meat, and you should put the major points you want to give further details about in this part of your presentation. These main points should be written in simple easy to understand language so that they are easily recognized and remembered when people leave your talk or presentation. These points need support, they will need to be explained, clarified, and have proof (case studies, statistics and testimonials). These can come in the form of specific details, by way of comparisons, examples, and demonstrations.

Here are some steps you can take to make the main points of the content of your presentation memorable:

Limit the number of points you cover, this will also be dictated by the amount of time you have been allocated to do your presentation.

You can also structure your content so that you cover the most important points either at the beginning or end this will depend on what your purpose of your presentation is.

Finally make the main points be remembered by making up an acronym or rhyme.

Concluding Your Presentation

The way you close your presentation is very important. Your close should include a summary of the main points and ideas covered in presentation and depending on the intended purpose of your presentation include an appropriate call to action.

Here are some closing ideas:

Issue a challenge to your audience. make an appeal to your audience to take action. E.g. To support your cause, hire you, buy your product or service or join your community.

Ask your audience to visualize their future. Get them to see themselves in the future and how their newly gained knowledge has impacted their life or how their failure to take action will have a negative impact on them, their families, social life, environment, society etc.

Include memorable quotations that relate to the topic you have presented also work well or simply referring your audience to the introduction, i.e. return the audience to your opening statement and leaving them with that thought.

Having a strong conclusion is important and because you want to make it memorable your conclusion or close should be well thought out. You want to end your presentation with a strong close and produce and have a positive effect on your audience.

In my opinion, it is very much about having a well practiced presentation. Practice does make perfect. Remember *"Every master was once a disaster!"*

Places To Speak At:

So where do you get speaking gigs? Here are a few suggestions: You can approach Chamber Of Commerce, Community Groups and Associations, Meetup groups, Schools, Public Libraries, Trade Associations, Business Networking Groups, Special Interest and Hobby Groups or Toast Masters International. You can run your own webinars, podcasts, web TV shows or present on other peoples podcasts and web TV shows.

Promote that you are a speaker on your relevant social media profiles. LinkedIn is a good platform to do this on.

Public speaking is a great way to gain credibility in your field and put you in a position of authority. You have the opportunity to connect with, entertain, educate and inform and persuade an audience on your topic of expertise. Public speaking will also present opportunities for you to advance your career, elevate your personal status, your business, your brand, and done properly be well rewarded financially. It will improve your confidence and a build a network of contacts for you to help or call upon.

Get out there, be heard, deliver your message and SPEAK OUT!

Bonus Chapter 2 - Media Exposure With Press Releases

In this chapter we are going to go over the power of using press releases. I am going to share with you my story and the exposure it gave me for one of my former businesses. You will see why they are so powerful and why they should be part of your marketing arsenal.

A press release also known as news release or media release is a written communication sent to the media for the purpose of announcing something newsworthy. Press releases can come in the form of online press releases that are distributed through the internet and offline press releases that are sent via fax, email and even via post to media outlets.

Press releases are great way of getting positive publicity for your business and your brand. They will assist in gaining you instant credibility and exposure to the masses. You will be seen as an expert and an authority in your market, niche or industry. Other benefits include the visitors or traffic that they will send to your web site or place of business and in effect increasing leads and sales.

Press releases work because it's been written by a third party and in most cases any reviews or articles written about you or your business can come across as an endorsement.

Most businesses don't use the power of press release because they think you have to be a great writer to produce a media release or must have the contacts or know people that are journalists. This is simply not the case and I will demonstrate this now to you by telling you my story.

106 New Customers in 24 Hours

It was the month of May 2004 where I decided to write a press release to gain more exposure for our salsa dance school. I have always been an avid student of anything to do with marketing and I was reading an article one day on how to use press releases to get more exposure and sales for your business. I thought I would give writing a press release a try and the results absolutely "gob smacked me." More on this in a moment.

I have never considered myself a great writer, in fact I am the son of two Italian immigrants and even though I was born in Australia. My first language was Italian and really only learnt to speak English when I started primary school. My English was OK to reasonable but I was never going to a literary. Anyway, I thought long and hard about how I was going to get more people to my salsa dance classes. I came up with the idea of a free four week salsa dance course. I named the course *"Salsa To The Max"* I wrote the press release with the title:

FREE *four week "Salsa to the Max" dance course will have you feeling great, keeping fit, having fun as well as give YOU the skills to enter the social dance floor with ease.*

In the press release I mentioned that salsa dancing was taking the world by storm and described the benefits learning salsa would provide. One thing I did which is aligned to the theme of this book was I stood on the shoulders of popular movies that had come out early in the year, which were Along Came Polly - with Ben Stiller and Jennifer Aniston and Havana Nights, the sequel to Dirty Dancing which featured a cameo appearance by the late Patrick Swayze. These movies featured salsa dancing in them (*the scene in Along Came Polly where Ben Stiller goes salsa dancing is hilarious!)*. I made mention of these movies in my release and added the details of where we were going to hold the course and a little about our salsa dancing experience.

After writing the press release I called the major radio stations, newspapers and local news papers in Perth and asked them the name of the person I had to submit my release to and whether they wanted me to fax it in or send it via email. The majority of the stations and newspapers were happy for me to send it via email, with an accompanying cover letter. The process of writing and sending off my press release took a whole of two hours of my time.

The Result:

I was contact by a major radio station to be a part of their breakfast show, which at the time was the prime show in Perth. I was asked to be interviewed on the show the day before my free salsa course started. I was on for about a whole two minutes. In that time they (the DJ's) made fun of my name and wanted to know if I looked like Fabio, the Italian male model who featured on the cover of Mills and Boons romance novels. It was a fun interview. They gave my business a plug on air and told the listeners about the free course and where it was held. I gave out my mobile (cell) phone number on air and I couldn't believe the response. My phone went into melt down - I was still retrieving messages late into the night from my message bank.

We turned up to teach the course and we couldn't believe the amount of people that had showed up waiting outside. We had people that drove over forty kilometres to take our free four week course. Eighty nine people came as a result of the radio interview and seventeen came from two local newspapers our business was mentioned in. It was fantastic. I was able to put these people on my mailing list so that I could market to them in the future. After the four weeks, I had thirty people join my full ten week course and out of those thirty seventeen of them took my classes, courses and workshops for the next three years. Not bad for two hours work. I don't say this to brag but to make you realise the power of press releases and why you should use them also.

I used this strategy on another occasion where I was starting classes in a new area, It was to teach salsa on the beach. My approach this time was different, I contacted the local community newspaper for that area and asked to speak to a journalist for the paper. I had a conversation with journalist and told him what I had in mind. He asked me to send in a news release to him. A few days later I received a call from the photographer from the community newspaper asking if I could organise to bring a few dancers to the beach for a photo shoot as we were going to be featured on the front page of the local community newspaper. We were excited and the photo shoot was fun. The photo they were going to use had us dancers dressed like we would be dressed on a dance floor but set on the beach and as if it was planned a surfer with his surf board at the time we were being photographed was shot in the background of our photo. It looked amazing.

The next week the news paper was published. I made sure I got a few copies of it. When I looked at the front page ,we weren't featured as we were promised. It was a feature of the legendary band, The Beach Boys as they were going to be in Perth doing a concert. We were pushed further back in the paper. The journalist called me and explained that we had been dropped from the front page headline because of the Beach Boys concert. It was down to timing. I didn't mind, even though we were a little disappointed. We still got a good write up and were able to attract over thirty people to the course.

Above I have described a few scenarios of how I have used press releases. These were all examples of using offline press releases. So what about online releases what are the differences? Apart from the obvious in that they are distributed online. Online press releases in my opinion are used to connect with and influence audiences in your related market, niche or industry topic on social media platforms and forums.

Online press releases should be optimized (SEO) using words (keywords that describe your business) for your business so that you get search engine exposure. For example: If I was a painter in my home town of Perth. I could write a press release on the colour trends for 2015. The title of the release might be "Perth Painter Let's You In On The "In" Colour Trends For 2015." This press release could possible rank well in the search engines for the search term Perth Painter. Online press releases allow you to link back to your website. The more press releases you publish with a link back to your website, will act like a vote for your website and will help your site to rank.

I think the key take away is when writing an online press release is to write for the search engines so you can be found. Keyword research is important here. Use the Google keyword planner to help you search for terms the public put in to find your business. Also be sure to put yourself in the shoes of your prospective customers and write down what search terms they would use to find your business. Google Keyword Planner will also display the number of searches for the term i.e. Perth Painter and give related terms and their search volumes as well. There are both free and paid online press release sites. If don't have a budget use the free ones otherwise use both.

Your Steps To Writing Your Press Release

Your press release shouldn't be a sales pitch. It should be newsworthy and you need to have a news angle. Here are some suggestions on some angles you can base your press releases on :

Is your story trendy or on a trending topic? - (Check Google trends and hot searches)

Is it controversial or Scandalous ?

Is it a human interest story ?

Is it a feel good story?

Is it something new?

Once you have established your angle of your press release you need to include in the body of your release:

The Who? - The name of your business, your name, which target market (client profile) does your news affect or benefit?

The What? - What is the announcement?, What is new?, What is the problem and or the solution?

The Why? - Why is your news important, Why is your news different or unusual?

The Where - Where is the news happening, Which geographic location or place ?

The When? - When is it happening ? This is great if you are doing a launch ,fundraiser or another event. What day, date and time ?

The How? How did this come about?

Here are the elements to include in your press release:

Contact details: Name, Address, Contact Numbers & Email Address and Website address placed in the top left hand corner.

Then underneath your contact details write: MEDIA RELEASE OR PRESS RELEASE and include the date you have sent the release on the same line but to the right hand side.

Then you need to write the term: FOR IMMEDIATE RELEASE followed by your HEADLINE to grab the attention of the media. Sometimes a press release will be distributed early and embargoed which means that, the media are requested not to make the story public until a particular date and time. If this is the case, you simply write it as EMBARGO: and put in the date and time.

Then you write the location and date of your story followed by the opening paragraph which should catch the media's attention and entice them to read further.

You can use bullet points as it does make it easier to read . Include quotes as part of your press release and write it in the third person for example: *Salsa instructor, Fabio said:* "*Salsa dancing will bring another dimension to your life in that it will connect you with many diverse people from around the globe and a skill that you will have for the rest of your life."*

Remember to cover the who, what, why, where, when and how as mentioned previously. Try keep your media release to one page. Conclude your release with ### - this a traditional way of telling the media that the release has ended.

> I have included in your bonus area a copy of my press release that I used to attract 106 new customers. Simply visit: **www.OnlineGiantsBook.com** to download it.

Using Media Kits.

Media Kits are great way to get your press release published. Accompanying your media release you can include a bio/fact sheet about you which include some back ground information about you and suggested interview questions for your media source or reporter. You can also include images and pictures. You can use this to your advantage as you are doing most of the work for the reporter. You are giving them the content for their story. In essence you are making it easy for them.

Press releases are very powerful. This chapter was an overview of how you can use the power press releases. Press releases are versatile in that if you have a good angle they can be used to get you, your business and your brand great exposure both online and offline. Keep in mind that you are not going to get interviewed or have your story printed all the time. But one thing I found is that the more you do use this strategy the more chance you will have succeeding with it.

Bonus Chapter 3 - Go To The People And Their Power

In this chapter I am going to give an overview on how to use social media to start building your authority in your market. The likes of Facebook, YouTube, LinkedIn, Google plus to name a few are online social media giants that have millions if not billions of people that engage multiple times on a daily basis on their sites. They allow you to reach their audience via their platforms so you too can connect and start a dialogue with your audience.

Your objective with your social media is to reach your audience by proving quality posts that educates, informs, entertains your market and build your know like and trust factor.

The world is social. I read recently that 63% of the world population use social media in one form or another. In a world population of over 7.2 Billion that's about 4.5 Billion people. That's massive, and that's why it's important in the first instance to find out which social media sites your audience frequent and are connected to.

Here are some figures on the amount of users of the more popular social media sites:

Google Plus : 300 Million active monthly users

Facebook: 1.35 billion monthly active users.

Twitter: 271 million monthly active users

YouTube: 1 Billion monthly active users

Instagram: 200 Million monthly active users

Pinterest : 70 Million users

LinkedIn: 300 Million registered users

Participating and engaging in conversation with the social media sites where your market is present is a great way (and a free way) to promote the name of your brand and business and attract and build strong relationships with customers and those that visit your social media business profiles and pages. Social media is great for finding out what your customers think about your products and or service offerings.

You need to have a social media strategy; an end game. You should have a plan of what objective/s you would like to achieve with your strategy. One idea that comes to mind is to move your audience from the social networking site to your email list to build a database that you can communicate with and market to. It's important that you put some thought into how you are going to do this and have an action plan to execute your strategy.

In regards to a few tips about using social media, it's important that you have your profile and your social media accounts looking professional and aligned to the target markets you serve. What I mean by that is that they know what your business is about by just looking at your profile and also in the language that you use in communicating with them, including any jargon that's relevant to your industry or market.

Your goal should really be to build fans and followers, and as mentioned before, get them to move across to your email list and your database so that you can communicate with them.

It's important that the content that you do post is there to inform, educate, and entertain your fans and followers. Make the content so good that they want to share it and pass it on to their other social platforms.

Remember start off by optimizing one platform at a time. Don't try to do everything and post on everything at the same time. It will just really lead to overwhelm and paralysis and when there is paralysis there is no action.

Take one platform at a time, and it's important to remember choose only the social media platforms that are relevant to where your audience is present and engaged. You don't have to be on all of them.

As a general rule, you'd want to be posting at least three times per day per platform. That's why it's important to get one platform up and running at a time. The good thing is that you can create content way in advance and also schedule it out. You can also use a social media management company, like SocialMediaWorldWide.com to manage your social media for you or a service like Traffic Geyser 2.0 and Instant Customer that allows you to schedule your social media posts out in advance, and help you automate the process. Here you will create your content in advance and then drip feed it to your audience over time.

What sort of content should you actually post on your social media? Well, we've talked in the previous chapters about your videos, your podcasts and even the content of your book. Why not drip feed the content that you've already created as your social media post? You can run contests, you can run polls and surveys. These are all ways to engage and interact with your audience.

You can also talk about trends and topics that your current audience are also engaged with at the moment. This is always a very good strategy.

Your posts should also ask your audience to take action as well, whether it'll be to subscribe to one of your podcasts, like your page, share your content, subscribe to your YouTube channel or simply send them to your website. Remember that there needs to be a bit of a balance because people don't go on these social platforms really to be sold or pressured. They are there, to be informed, to be educated, and to be entertained, so don't pepper them with calls to action all the time. It should probably be about an 80/20 split, 80% of great content and 20% of asking them to subscribe.

In closing, I really want you to harness the power of the social media. Use it wisely. Use it to promote your business and brand by giving great value, great content and engaging with your audience so they trust you enough to reach out to you to help them because in their eyes and minds they regard you as the expert that can solve their problems.

Bonus Chapter 4 - What's Your Service Like?

In this chapter we are going to talk about how important providing excellent customer service is for your business and how you can use high quality service delivery to set yourself apart from your competition in your market.

But first I want to tell you a story....

After graduating from high school in the late eighties I got my first job working in a bank as a bank teller . The bank that employed me was one of the our "BIG FOUR" banks that are based here in Australia. It was very competitive, all the banks offered the same banking products, they were all very competitive with their interest rates. The bank I worked for was rated as the number two bank in Australia at the time. We were striving to be number one. So with all things being equal we (*the banks management*) set out to be the number one bank in Australia. They achieved this a short time later (*within twelve months*).

Can you guess how they became the number one bank? It was through customer service; superior customer service. Management looked at what our competition was doing, and improved on it by bringing in and investing in experts to put systems in place and train our staff Australia wide.

I am going to ask you a few questions and I want you to take a few moments to reflect on these questions and be honest with your answers. "How do you treat your customers?" "How do you treat and engage with them compared to your competitors?" "If you have staff, have you trained them in effective customer service?" and "How responsive are you to your clients needs?" "What can you do better or improve on?" "Do you have a system in place for customer service?" "Do you keep in touch after the sale or after you have delivered your service?" "How do you handle complaints?" Please remember that bad news travels fast and it has been said that people who experience bad service will tell on average about thirteen others about their bad experience. Also let's not forget how quickly things spread on social media! *"Remember if you have no customers, you have no business* **RIGHT?**"

This chapter was written as an added value piece and I was fortunate enough to get Josh Oakey from The Customer Service Movement; who is a Customer Service Coach and Consultant to agree to share part of our interview we recently did on customer service, including how you can use customer service to set yourself apart from your competitors and how to increase your profits through service excellence.

> To get the full audio interview simply register your details at **OnlineGiantsBook.com**

Here is what spoke about on our call:

Fabio : *Josh, why is customer service so important?*

Josh: Fabio, someone once said to me that people don't just buy a product from a business, they buy from people. They buy from people that they know, like and trust and that's the key to customer service. Anyone can sell a product, but there's only, I wouldn't say a select few, but there are certain businesses that do the customer service better than others, that can continue to sell the same product to the same people and new people. Without the customer service you might get one sale, but you'll never get that repeat sales.

Fabio :*Can you give the listeners some advice or tips in regards to handling an irate or an angry customer? What's the best way to deal with an angry or irate customer in your opinion?*

Josh: Yeah. I've said it before, it's silence. It's really just turning off your mouth and listen to what they're actually arguing about. Like I said before, it's usually other things that you've got no control over, and that's what they're really annoyed at. You've sort of just pushed them over the edge by a service defect or a product that's not working to what they expect. When you're trying to handle that irate or angry customer, it's really about showing, if it's in person, being very open with your body language. Not crossing the arms and rolling the eyes and all the rest of those beautiful things that teenagers do to parents.

Need to be very open and listen and then you don't have to sympathize, you just need to empathize where their position is coming from, and then address what they've actually said, not just try and waffle back and come up with excuses. Accept what they're feeling, and then have a solution in the back of your mind that you can present to them there and then, if possible.

Fabio, that one always works, especially if you've got a 15, 16 year-old casual in your business. Not that they're silly, they might just not have that maturity to deal with that situation properly at that stage. They need to be aware that they say, "Thank you for your feedback. I just need to go and get my manager, or a more senior person on the floor and I'll explain to them your situation and then we'll deal with it together." It's not just playing handball along because no one likes that.

The same thing happens in call centres. If you ever rung an organization and you need to complain and all that's happening is you bounce from department to department. You have to explain yourself 5 times, that is so frustrating as a customer. You can alleviate that by listening and getting the full picture and then passing that information on for the customer. That's how I'd deal with it.

Sometimes you don't have the answer and you need to say, "Look, I've taken it all onboard and I'll get back to you tomorrow when we're all calmed down." That might not help, you're trying to alleviate the problem straight away, but big problems sometimes need a bit more investigation than an on-the-minute split decision.

Fabio : *In your experience, what are some of the biggest mistakes that businesses make with their service delivery?*

Josh: I guess your biggest experiences come from being a consumer, don't they?

I work with businesses, so I see it from their point of view, and I've worked in a lot. The ones that stick with you are as that consumer. Some of the mistakes that I see from a consumer's point of view, it's just acknowledgement and appreciation that you've gone out of your way to go into a business or visit their website, and there just doesn't seem to be any appreciation there. Just a thank you, or thanks for coming. How can we help? What is it that you're actually after? Not trying to sell your product straight away because it might not actually fit their solution. Can I tell you a story about our chauffeur business?

Fabio : Yes, please do.

Josh: We have a chauffeur business, which many people think that we do limousines, which we don't. We do executive sedans. While we get a lot of inquiries as to, "Do you do a limousine service?" Even though we're clear on our site that we don't, you still get that influx of requests. We could just say, "No, we don't do limousines," and hang up the phone. What we do is refer them to our competitors or our affiliates who do limousines.

The reason we do that is because they have come to us. They have taken the time to pick up the phone or write us an email and say, "Can you help?" We are able to help, but we're not going to profit from it. What we've been able to do is not only capture a phone number, an email and an name who we can market to later, but we've also been able to point them in the direction they were coming to us for. We've endorsed our affiliates or our competitors to be able to provide that service. We've done all we can in that little transaction, but we've built a bit of trust with that person who's contacted us. Seventy-five percent of the time they'll come back to us for another quote within a month.

Fabio : Wow, that's a very interesting stat. Seventy-five percent of the time, that's quite a high strike rate.

Josh: It is. We're very proud of that, that even though we're not giving them the service that we would like to in the actual product sense, we've done our best from our customer service viewpoint. The reason I told you that story is that other businesses would just say, "No, we don't do limousines," and then hang up the phone. We've been able to create a good service experience and then future business from that. I'd say that's one of the biggest mistakes. Being a bit small-minded and not looking at the big picture for repeat business.

Fabio :*Are there any differences in the way that you deliver customer service online compared to offline?*

Josh: I think the biggest difference, is that the online world is changing every day. The way that you respond needs to keep up with that change. The customer service online ... I'm not sure about you when you shop online, do you get that feeling that everything needs to be very quick and immediate? If you don't .... you don't get that response, well why didn't I just get in the car and go to another business? I think that customer service from an online point of view needs to be solid and very structured in the response time. Automating replies to any queries needs to be seamless.

It's crazy, you get new content for customer service every single day. On Friday I was trying to contact a very large social media planning website. I won't tell you who it is, but I needed to downgrade my package. I couldn't find a phone number. I couldn't explain it well enough in my email that this had to happen because I've already been charged for it, I need it refunded. I couldn't find a phone number to get into contact with their accounts department. I think that is one of the key areas that online businesses need to keep in mind, that even though we like to shop online as consumers, we still like some personal touch when we feel like it's urgent, or it needs to be fixed. That call centre is very, very important in my opinion. You need to give your customers another way of contacting you other than just email. It frustrated me a great deal. That's one of my experiences.

Yeah, huge differences between your online and offline, but the core value is still the same. Answer your customer's problems and provide them with a solution and do it in a timely manner.

Fabio : *Josh, how could you use customer service to set your business apart from your competitors?*

Josh: Yeah. The first part of that is, you need to know your competitors. I was talking to a client the other day and I said, "So, who's your competitor?" He said, "I don't have any." Well, that's a great industry. Can I become your competitor? Let's do this. You need to be open to, you've got competitors no matter what market, what niche, what industry you're in. Just because you do something slightly different doesn't mean you don't have competitors.

I guess how you can use the customer service to set you apart from your competitors is to know your customers better than your competitors do. Find out when their birthday is. Do they have a pet dog, are they married, are they single? Then start becoming a part of their lives. That sounds quite obtrusive, but if you've got that information then you can start talking to your customers as they're your friends, not as if they're your customers still. We have a very different way of talking. If your competitors are not doing that, they're going to come back to you because they like you, they trust you and they believe in what you're doing.

Share your personal life with them as well. I was listening to a lady on a podcast not long ago, and she said she wanted to cleanse her list. I thought, "Here we go. What's this all about?" She sent out a very personal email telling of a life event that had just happened. I think her and her partner had a big argument or fallout, and she just went into great detail about it. She said, "I lost 20% of my list." Now, that sounds pretty scary, but what she kept was 80% of people who had a stronger relationship with her now. Then she found that from then on, her actual list increased because people started referring them to her, family and friends, just to join the list to hear about this lady's personal life. Not in a drama sort of a way, but they could trust her because she was just a person. It wasn't a business front, it was a person behind the business.

I found that to be quite insightful. If you can relate better to your customers than your competitors ,people will stay with you and talk about you more.

Fabio : *What sort of things can businesses do to keep on top of their customer service delivery?*

Josh: There's some easy ways and then there's some 'think outside the box' sort of scenarios. Mystery shops are always a great way of doing it if you're in an offline business. You can employ companies or you can ask family and friends to mystery shop your business. Provide them with a checklist of what you expect out of your team. Then they come in and do a shop and they can provide you feedback of how the staff had actually performed. I'd do that across your whole business, actually, in your business, phone support and your website to how easy it is to get around. As business owners and as managing stores in the past, I've found that you can get a little bit shop blind from time to time. You'll say, "Oh, don't worry about painting that fixture just yet. We'll get to it, or it's a bit too expensive at this stage." If you invite a new set of eyes in to mystery shop your business, that'll come out.

Then it's just all about systems, daily, monthly, fortnightly checks. I've spoken before about making sure that someone crawls through your website once a month to make sure all the forms are all working. We had an experience with our chauffeur business very recently that our contacts seemed to dry up, our inquiries. I thought well, "What's going on here?" I'd only just checked the site and when we'd played around at the backend of our website, one of the boxes weren't ticked. We weren't actually getting notified of any of the inquires. They were all coming through, but unfortunately our email software wasn't telling us. We had a bad customer experience in our business. I'm the first to say I make mistakes as well. What we then had to do, do you mind me telling you how we fixed it?

Fabio :Yeah, please do, please share.

Josh: I was devastated that we'd made people wait 7 days before we got back to them because we guarantee 24 hours. I sent out an email, "I'm so sorry and embarrassed. Here is the information that you need. If you can find it in your hearts to contact us again, I'll be happy to provide more information for you." From that we had 10 contacts that hadn't heard from us. Eight of them actually sent an email back to me and said, "Don't worry, it's fine. Thanks for the information." One of them booked. The other one said, "No, it's out of our price range."

That gave me confidence that if you actually accept that you've made a mistake and you tell people like it is, they forget very, very quickly what you did to mess up. We accepted that we'd made the mistake and then we went to fix it. I expected them to say, "Oh well, too bad. You had your chance." It was humbling for us to know that, okay, we've messed up and then they actually accepted our apology, which was very good. I'd say that to all the listeners today that if you make a mistake, be very clear and open about what mistake you've made. Accept that some people won't be happy about your mistake, but there'll be a large portion that say, "Thanks, you're human. We get it and we know that you'll try and fix everything from now on."

Fabio :Yeah. That's an excellent story there, Josh, that you said. I've been on the receiving end of something similar to that. For someone, like you did, to take responsibility, that actually, I think, instils that trust as well. Starts to build up their trust by you apologizing.

We were taught, as kids, if you make a mistake, you apologize. You try to fix it. At times, I think as humans, we tend to overcomplicate things. Just simply saying, "Sorry. This shouldn't have happened." As you did, provide a response. I've found that most people are understanding. I really like that story and I think it makes that point of what you just said. Very good.

Josh: Yeah. I guess it's just keeping on top of your customer service. It's being aware of what's happening in your business. You set up the systems and checks within your business for each part of your customer service delivery. Your website, you might put in that every 3 months you want to change it because it might not be relevant anymore, because the copy might need to change. It might be a seasonal thing. Don't just do it when you think you've got time. Plan it out and say, "Right, in 3 months we're going to change it. So, a month out we need to start looking at what our customers are asking us and then put it in place on that date." Work to the rule, be systemized in your business and then your customer service will flow on and your customers will know what to expect.

I want to thank Josh Oakey for his generosity and the time he has taken out of busy schedule to contribute to this book. If you'd like to get more information on how you can increase your profits through customer service simply visit Josh's site: www.thecustomerservicemovement.com.au

Moving Forward

I think you will agree you've been given some really great information in this book. We have covered 7 ways that you can leverage the power of the big brands online, our online giants to position you as an authority in your market or industry. The strategies and tactics you've uncovered in this book are very powerful and will only come to fruition for you by you taking action.

Implement the strategy that is going to best suit your business in the first instance and then move on to the next. I want to stress that to be effective in using your chosen strategy it's really important you know who your audience and competition is as we discussed in chapter one. This part of the equation coupled with delivering great content will stack the odds in your favour at succeeding.

Register For Your Complimentary Webinar And Bonuses

Remember to register for your **FREE** webinar, updates and bonus resource guides by visiting:

www.OnlineGiantsBook.com

Join Our Special Online Giants Book Facebook Group

I invite you to join our Facebook group just for readers like you who want to take their businesses to the next level. In this group we'll be sharing our successes, more digital marketing tips, great content and strategies so that you and the entire members of our group can continue to grow your businesses. This is also a fantastic group for making contacts with like minded people. It's a safe space where you can ask for other members input on ideas or projects you are working on. This group is there to encourage you and help you with any questions you may have.

I look forward to welcoming you to our exclusive group.

Get The Breakthrough You Need

We have covered a lot information in this book, which sometimes can cause overwhelm. So to help you out I have decided to offer you, a special, **"Business Positioning Breakthrough" Coaching Session** where we'll work together to:

Create a clear vision for your ultimate business success, identify how to best position your business for this success and the "ideal lifestyle" you'd like your business to offer you.

Uncover hidden challenges that may be hindering the growth of your business and keeping you chasing your tail and feeling overwhelmed.

You will leave this session renewed, re-energized, and inspired to turn your business into a highly profitable, automated and revenue-generating machine through the powerful strategies I will share with you.

If you'd like to take advantage of this very special, very limited, and totally **FREE 30 minute "Business Positioning Breakthrough" coaching session**, email me at onlinegiantsbook@gmail.com to organize it.

Finally I want to say another BIG "Thank You" for purchasing and reading my book. I encourage you to take action and I wish you much success.

Wishing you good things,

Fabio Mastrocola

PS: If you have any questions, successes or stories you'd like to share please email me at:

onlinegiantsbook@gmail.com

About The Author:

Fabio Mastrocola is a Digital Marketing Coach. He has a passion for helping small to medium enterprises embrace the ever evolving digital landscape to help them position their businesses as an authority in their market converting more customers and creating more cash flow for their business by using the power of Digital Multicast Marketing".

Fabio lives in Perth ,Western Australia with his wife Rita.

As business owner himself Fabio understands the importance of positioning you and or your brand as the expert in your market or field. He has helped and advised small to medium businesses in a variety of industries including Real Estate, Manufacturing, Construction and Medical Emergency Training.

Fabio has a passion for coaching, educating and inspiring business owners to harness the opportunities digital multicast marketing will provide them so that they too can reach and live their dreams.

With a wealth of knowledge and experience in business development and sales and marketing he is committed to taking businesses to the next level so that they can enjoy better results and success.

Fabio can be reached at: onlinegiantsbook@gmail.com.

www.ingramcontent.com/pod-product-compliance
Lightning Source LLC
Chambersburg PA
CBHW051714170526
45167CB00002B/657